ISBN 978-1-332-16073-0
PIBN 10292823

1 MONTH OF
FREE
READING

at

www.ForgottenBooks.com

By purchasing this book you are eligible for one month membership to ForgottenBooks.com, giving you unlimited access to our entire collection of over 700,000 titles via our web site and mobile apps.

To claim your free month visit:

www.forgottenbooks.com/free292823

Similar Books Are Available from
www.forgottenbooks.com

THE MYSTIC TEST BOOK

OR THE

MAGIC OF THE CARDS.

*Giving the Mystic Meaning of these Wonderful and Ancient Emblems in their
Relationship to the Heavenly Bodies, Under all Conditions; With Rules
and Processes for Reading or Delineating the Emblems.*

COPIOUSLY ILLUSTRATED.

Written and Compiled Under the Authority of the Mystic Brotherhood,

BY

OLNEY H. RICHMOND,

GRAND MASTER OF THE INNER TEMPLE OF THE ANCIENT
ORDER OF THE MAGI.

Author of "TEMPLE LECTURES." "RELIGION OF THE STARS," Etc.

CHICAGO, ILL., U. S. A.

Important Notice.

This work is fully protected by copyright according to law, No. 4723 Y, issued January 23d, 1893. Every table, illustration and definition is copyrighted, and all persons are warned against re-printing them or any part of them, under penalty of the law, which will be strictly enforced.

The owner of this book has signed an agreement whereby said owner is bound to not lend the work, or allow the use of the same to extend to persons outside his own immediate family, nor to allow any person to copy, nor obtain a copy of any of the rules, processes or engravings therein.

This rule is designed as a protection to said owner, as well as to the author and the good of the Order. It is intended to prevent the wearing out and soiling of the book and the gathering of deleterious influences and magnetism by the promiscuous handling and loaning about the neighborhood that most books on occult subjects receive.

★ ★ ★

This prohibition need not be construed so strictly as to prevent outsiders *seeing* the book, or even reading it in your home or presence. If your friend or acquaintance wishes to procure a copy, an order blank will always be sent, on application to us.

OLNEY H. RICHMOND,

-     CHICAGO, ILL.

iii

Dedication.

To the friends of our secret order, within the sacred fold and without. To those who are regular attendants at our Grand Temple and unto those whose duties call them elsewhere. To all those who, having charity and kindness in their hearts and harmony in their souls, are willing to yield themselves to the work of regeneration and advancement, with that energy characteristic of true mystics. To those who have an affinity for the good, the pure and the true, as well as the spiritual advancement and development which enables them to comprehend the mysteries of the infinite and majestic universe.

To the faithful ones in Temple or Court, faithful through fire, through water, through earth, through air, to the East, to the West, to the South and to the North, with all and through all.

This volume is respectfully dedicated by the author,

Olney H. Richmond.

iv

Introduction.

The publication of this work was, we might say, forced upon us by the demand, before even a page of manuscript was prepared for the press. The demand was caused by members of the Temple, who recognized the necessity of a printed text book, from which they could study the meanings of the cards and their indications under the seven planets.

These brothers and sisters naturally wished to perfect themselves in emblem reading as rapidly as possible, and they could not so perfect themselves, without a full and complete set of tables that they could study and refer to at will. The next trouble that arose was the question of expense, as, aside from the printing, engraving, binding, electrotyping and matters of that kind, the author's time was, and is now so valuable that the item far overbalances those mentioned.

It was finally decided that the most feasible plan, was to get out enough copies to supply more than our immediate membership and to sell them to outsiders under certain restrictions.

We only intended, at first, to get out a book of about one hundred and sixty pages to be bound in cloth. But the generous subscriptions forwarded to us caused us to change our mind and we began writing additional copy. We are so occupied with Temple work, that this extra labor, together with superintending the publication and proof reading, has caused considerable delay beyond the time first set. We are sorry for this, but it could not well be avoided.

Please remember, friends, that the price charged for this book is *not for the size*, nor the binding, nor the number of pages, but for the matter itself. The emblem delineation department is alone worth more than the price charged for the entire work. We have placed much other information in the book in addition to the tables of readings, in order to compensate our kind friends for the patient waiting and the numerous subscriptions they have procured for us.

We certainly undertook the work at a time when the conditions were extremely unfavorable. We have been overrun with work in the Grand Temple, and down town shops engaged in the lines connected with book making are all full of World's Fair work. At last we have overcome the obstacles and here is the book which we hope will please you.

Respectfully and fraternally yours,

THE AUTHOR.

Index.

Index.

INDEX

CHAPTER I.

The Little Book.

"And when the Seven Thunders had uttered their voices, I was about to write; but I heard a voice from heaven, saying unto me, seal up those things, uttered by the Seven Thunders, and write them not."

"And I took the *little book* out of the Angel's hand and devoured it; and to my taste it was sweet as honey; but as soon as I had devoured it, it became bitter unto my inside."

"And he said unto me, you must prophesy again before many peoples and nations and tongues and kings."

(*Correct translation of Rev. X, 4, 10 and 11.*)

DEAR READER:

AS a text to this work read and consider the above, and it would be as well to read the entire tenth chapter of Revelations, for the whole book is a mystic one.

If you are able to "read between the lines" you will comprehend that the "little book" that was capable of voicing the "7 thunders," that is, the voices of the seven planets, was the only and original test-book of the mystic brotherhood. Did you or did anyone ever know of another book that was always made small enough to "hold in the hand?"

At last the utterances of the little book which was sealed

for a time, are to be opened unto the gaze of men. At last its wonders are to be unfolded partially that we may prophesy before many peoples.

Read Chapter V of Revelations.

No other book that ever had an existence upon our planet, has within itself the wonderful properties that are indubitably attached to this little book. No other "book" has been so "sealed" with hidden emblematic meanings as to defy all attempts to "open" its pages.

It is the *oldest* book known and it existed long before the modern written languages were thought of.

Its history extends so far back into the dim recesses of the past, that we must *per force* ask our readers to take circumstantial evidence as to its early history and uses.

THE ORIGIN OF PLAYING CARDS.

The ancient origin and uses of "playing cards," which is the name they have been called by since the XIV Century has been shrouded in mystery, and their invention has been claimed by nearly every civilized nation upon the globe. The Chinese, Persians, Egyptians and several other ancient nations, claim the honor of their invention.

A pack of cards, said to be a thousand years old, is preserved in the Museum of the Royal Asiatic Society. It is also claimed that they have been known in India from *time immemorial.—(Cyc. Brit , Art. Cards.)*

When we find a certain invention claimed by a large number of Nations, scattered over our globe, in widely separated localities, we must conclude that none of them were the inventors, but on the contrary, obtained the inventions of some nation preceding them by many years.

This is actually the case with our test book, as well as with many other things used in modern times.

In addition to the great length of time that has elapsed since its invention, we have the fact to contend with, that the ancient and secret order that alone understood and used this mystic book, sedulously guarded the sacred emblems from the knowledge of the outside world. They were each and every one of them sworn not to "cut, carve, paint, mark or write them" upon any substance whatever, except for use in the Temples of the Mystic Brotherhood.

MYSTIC EMBLEMS.

The test book has been called by various names, among which the "Tarot Cards" appears in many ancient and modern works. Why they *are* tarot cards, will be seen when we come to the the tarot or magic square department. Many modern writers however, have been misled, by supposing that some of the many substitutes for the old genuine book are the real tarot cards. For instance; we find in a work called "*The Tarot of the Bohemians*," by "Papus," a large number of allusions to the test book, but strange to say, the writer substitutes a pack of 78 cards containing *Jewish and Catholic Symbols, Popes and Devils,* for the genuine cards. I quote from him a few passages.

"The Tarot pack of cards, transmitted by the Gypsies from generation to generation, is the primitive book of *ancient initiation.* This has been clearly demonstrated by Guillaume Postel, Court de Gebelin, Etteila, Eliphas, Levi and J. A. Vaillant. The key to its construction and application *has not yet been revealed,* as far as I know." (Preface to work.)

All very well, and true, if applied to *the* book. But what, may I ask, did the Magi of Egypt, or the Gypsies who inherited knowledge from them, have to do with Popes, Devils and "Angels of judgement" used in the bogus test book?

On pages 8 and 9, Papus says:—"The Gypsies possess a Bible, which has proved their means of gaining a livelihood, for it enables them to tell fortunes; yes; the game of cards called the Tarot, which the Gypsies possess, is the Bible of Bibles. It is the book of Thoth Hermes Trismegistus, the book of Adam, the book of primitive *Revelations of Ancient Civilizations.*

"Thus whilst the Freemason, an intelligent and virtuous man, has lost the tradition; while the priest, also intelligent and virtuous, has lost his esoterism; the Gypsy, although both ignorant and vicious, has given us the key which enables us to explain all the symbolism of the ages."

The work from which the above quotations are made, was handed to me by a friend, and upon reading the headings of chapters, I was delighted, thinking that a feast was in store, for I found such head lines as "The Astronomic Tarot;

Egyptian Astronomy; The Four Seasons; Application of the Tarot to Astronomy; Astronomy and Astrology; Fortune Telling by the Tarot," etc. But a perusal of the chapters under these head lines gave no light whatever upon occultism. The cards recognized by the author, being *worthless as a test book* and wholly useless as a *tarot book.*

Reader, do not be misled by any of the so-called occult works upon the subject. They are very numerous and all quote and re-quote from each other, but it is the old story of the "blind leading the blind," and we can see without glass es, behind all this dust throwing, the secret hand of the *great enemy of our order, and the enemy of science.*

The Egyptians were not the originators of the sacred Test Book. The only people that were ever so situated as to possess the knowledge and acquirements necessary for such a work, lived long anterior to the Egyptians.

That nation was the ATLANTIANS. This test book was the crystalization of ages upon ages of observation of the stars and planets, coupled with observations of the actions of mankind as known in that day.

Atlantis had an old and a grand civilization. She was the last remaining portion of a vast continent, that had existed for more than four hundred thousand years, where the great Atlantic Ocean now tosses its waves.

The engraving shows the remnant left, after untold thousands of years of wear and tear of the elements had degraded the continent and cast a great part of the detritus upon what afterwards became the Continent of America.

Upon a certain portion of this land, somewhat to the South-East of the geographical center thereof, existed highlands from which the land sloped in all directions by gentle undulations unto the sea. On this highland there were other much higher elevations in the shape of mountains, between which a most beautiful and fruitful valley reposed.

In the center of this valley, a small, nearly round lake reflected on its mirrored surface the mountain tops and the pinnacles of palaces and temples.

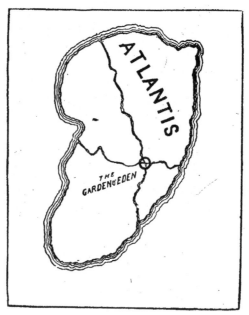

THE FINAL KINGDOM OF ATLANTIS.

Upon a large rock in the middle of the lake, the Atlantians builded the palaces of her Kings, gorgeous with costly stones and metals. Grand bridges lead to an embankment built entirely around the lake, except at four places to the N. S. E. and West, reserved for entrances by water. Upon this ring resided the Nobles of the Court and their families.

Outside the ring of land was a canal, used for purposes of pleasure, and from this, canals branched outward to a "belt-canal" surrounding the entire capitol. From the belt canal, other canals were cut between the mountains, North, South, East and West, where the water found its way to the sea by four rivers, as shown upon the map.

These rivers were kept constantly supplied with water by the copious rain-fall attracted by the mountain group about the capitol, and the good people residing in the four quarters of the island of Atlantis, used the four rivers as highways to their capitol and to transport their products thither.

Reader, Atlantis was the only place on this earth where four rivers flowed from one source. The only place where four Kings reigned in one capitol. The "Garden of Atlantis," as the island was called, for the inhabitants took rich earth and covered the rock many feet deep therewith, was planted with every tree and fruit to delight the palate or the eye of man.

In the midst of this garden stood the palace of the Kings, and the grand Temple of Wisdom, the Temple of her Priesthood, where the "Religion of the Stars" was the only religion known or practiced. This temple was the "tree of knowledge," against which the champions of revealed religion have cast their church thunderbolts and anathemas for ages and ages. "In the day that thou eatest thereof thou shalt surely die," is a formula that the church endeavored for ages and ages to make true. Thousands and millions of poor devoted followers of the truth who have ventured to taste the "forbidden fruit" have perished for it.

The first "Garden of Eden" was at the North Pole; the

l_{ast}, built in commemoration of the first, was on the island of Atlantis.

We have only given a rough sketch, of what could be expanded into a large book, but it is enough to start the mystic mind into making a study of the various proofs given in other works upon this subject.

About fifteen thousand years ago, Atlantis was in the height of her glory, with her colonies planted in all parts of the world, accessible to her commerce. Her strongest possessions, however, were situated in Egypt and South America, although she had cities as far north as the great lake that covered what is now Michigan and the chain of lakes surrounding that state.

For instance, the great city of Bab, stood 14,600 years ago, nearly where her modern representative, Chicago, now stands. Only the river, which is a small affair in this age, was then a wide and beautiful stream, flowing *from* the "Great-Lake-of-the-Northland" to the ocean, nearly 300 miles farther north than where New Orleans is now.

Nearly fourteen thousand nine hundred years ago, or about B. C. 13,000, the order of the Magi dedicated their first Temple in Egypt; the country which was destined to become the theater of the future exploits of the mystic brotherhood for thousands of years.

As long as Atlantis stood, she held the supreme jurisdiction over all parts of the earth, and Egypt was of course. subordinate to her in the occult and spiritual line.

But the time came a few hundred years later, when a terrible catastrophe hurled the rocky foundations from beneath Atlantis and in a day and night of the most heartrending and appalling crashes of earthquakes and thunders and lightenings, the 'doomed country sank beneath the waves of the Atlantic.

Nothing was left but a few mountain tops, to mark the place where a grand civilization had reigned. These mountain tops are now small islands, called the Azores, the central cluster of which mark the site of the ancient Capital.

CHAPTER II

The Religion of the Stars.

A RELIGION based upon the stars of heaven, which men had gazed upon for thousands upon thousands of years, was the most natural one that could be conceived.

Their knowledge of the planetary system was very great, for they had, by patient labor and striving, and by prolonged observation and calculation, not only gained a large amount of knowledge but they had, through their spiritual development, became possessed of means of gaining occult knowledge not obtainable through the physical, even with the aid of the best instruments of modern times.

Therefore the Ancient Magi taught a good, pure, scientific and rational religion, with symbolism of the grandest kind and a system of morals not surpassed by any modern system.

The world made a poor exchange when it accepted in lieu thereof, a man-made religion of gods, devils, heavens and hells; requiring an endless chain of rank absurdities to support the structure.

A BOOK OF SYMBOLS.

Any book written in a language other than symbolic, must in the course of time become nearly non-understandable

The "Trident". B.C. 21,000.

The Modern Seven.

The "Dipper". A.D. 1900.

through changes of language and meaning of words, to say nothing of loss through translations from translations, etc. But symbols are the same in all tongues and among all peoples.

The German maiden understands the meaning of a kiss

and gives it the same interpretation as does the English or Spanish maiden.

Thus the *heart* is an emblem of love the world over. The diamond an emblem of wealth.

The Ancient Magi understood this principle and they also understood the deeper hidden principle that underlies all symbolism, that is that there is a *spirit force* back of everything that exists; that the spirit force or astral light of a symbolic thing becomes a *fixed principle* through the mind and spirit force of man acting upon it for ages and ages.

A materialist cannot understand this, for his mind cannot grasp the meaning of spirit or mind.

When the writer was young, the coffin was stained and varnished usually only a few hours before being used, so that the peculiar smell came to be closely associated with death and funeral sermons.

I have conversed with many people regarding the sensations experienced by myself whenever I smell fresh varnish, and I find that nearly all whom I have compared notes with have recognized the same thing. A shudder and peculiar sinking of vibration connected with death. Thus, by the mere association for a few generations we have erected a symbol of death appealing to only one sense, smelling.

Emblems appealing to the eye have more power because they appeal by a higher vibration. The vibrations coming to the retina of the eye to produce the sensation of sight, run into hundreds of trillions per second, many times higher than those producing smell or taste. The symbols of taste are quite powerful in some directions, however, as most people have observed.

SYMBOLISM OF NUMBERS.

At the very foundation of all symbolism lie mathematics and geometry. In fact, the universe itself is built up, from the smallest particle seen under the compound microscope, to the largest sun or even Nebula, on exact geometrical and mathematical principles.

Men have simply followed Nature's lead in the symbolic use of numbers. The number seven is interwoven throughout the very warp and woof of Nature's handiwork. In all ancient books we find a divine plan of sevens extending through the pages. Genesis is written from first to last on a number plan. The great pyramids of Egypt are bristling throughout with a wonderful plan of mathematical and geometrical calculation, based upon knowledge of the grandest kind.

The basis of all numbers is *one*. The basis of all life is *one*. The basis of all that exists is *one*, the Universal Ego. But this number must be infinite, for the universe is infinite both in duration and extent. In fact the Universal Ego is made up of a countless number or entities, each in itself infinite in certain ways. Thus we can say, that there is an infinite number of suns, an infinite number of uninhabited worlds; an infinite number of inhabited worlds; an infinite number of satellites, in the universe. For *there can be no end to space,* and the same law that peoples one portion with countless numbers of heavenly bodies, must operate to produce them everywhere.

The Ancient Magi adopted, as their representation of infinity, a circle; for the very significant reason that a circle has no beginning or end and thus fulfills two of the conditions. They reasoned that the number *one* followed by an infinite number of circles would be a fit symbolical and mathematical representation of the *Infinite One.*

NUMBER OF THE INFINITE.

1OOOOOOOOOOOOOOO $+ \infty$

Later discoveries have proved that this is a wise thought and leads to many wonderful demonstrations of truth.

THE DIVINE OR SOUL NUMBER SEVEN.

The number 7 represents the soul in nature, and therefore becomes the center of all symbolic numbers, so to speak.

We find the sacred number interwoven into all the religious systems known on our planet, and the very warp and woof of Creation seem to bristle with sevens.

The sacred number of the Magi, and one that has been known in our symbolism as the strangest of all, is this

142857

Composed of twice 7: 4 times 7: 8 times 7 with the Ego added to the last figure.

It is a wonderful number, in a hundred different ways and is used in our temple work a great deal. We shall give some of the strange properties in various parts of this book.

It is evolved by dividing the number of the Infinite by the Soul number 7. Keep up the division to all eternity and you get nothing but the sacred number 142857 over and over. The wonders are best illustrated however with the emblems of the test book, as the reader will see further along.

The number 7 is the center of each suit of the test book, as can be best exemplified by the following

ILLUSTRATION IN SUIT OF HEARTS.

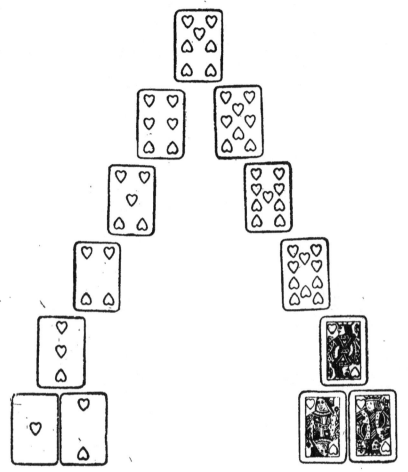

The mystic number can be represented in the emblems of knowledge as follows:

Change any card from right to left and you get a true product by some number.

Change the Ace of Clubs to the other end and you have the product of the sacred number by 3. Place the 7 to the left and you have the product by 5.

Suppose you wish to multiply the sacred number by 15.

Set down the number   142857

Take 7 to begin, thus   714285

Add together   2142855

which is 15 times the number.

But you could have taken 2 from the right hand figure and by placing it at the left you would have obtained the same result.

Multiply the sacred number by 7 and you obtain a product *all in nines*.

THE OCCULT PROPERTIES OF THE NO. 9.

The number nine is the representative of another phase of symbolism representing the duality of the physical, plus the deific seven.

Therefore we find in tarotology a wonderful blending of these two numbers in harmonious relations in thousands of ways.

So much has been written concerning the mystic qualities of the number nine, that it will be unnecessary to go into the subject at much length in this work. All products of nine and sums of products as well as products of sums have an Nth root of nine.

Many occult demonstrations have been given by means of a knowledge of the properties of this mystic nine.

Take any number, large or small, and place with it a reversal of itself and subtract one number from the other and the difference will always reduce to *nine*, and is always a multiple of that number.

Example—356781
Reversed—187653
Difference=169128=N 9

Take any number and subtract from it the sum of its own digits and the difference always has an Nth root—nine.

THE MYSTIC STAR TAROT.

One of the most wonderful combinations of the 7 and 9 properties is found in the Star Tarot of the Ancient Magi. This Star is composed of 2 equilateral triangles, one dark and one light, representing Darkness and Light of astronomy or the body and soul or physical and spiritual in nature.

Each triangle represents 3 from its geometrical quality United by multiplication, 3 times 3 or 9. The tarot, or Magic Square in the center is a 3 times 3 tarot with nine as its central figure.

Upon each point of the star is seen an emblem card from the Mystic Test Book, which taken by spot values represents the sacred number 142857 in regular order as the earth moves about the sun

The spot values of any two opposite emblems added together produce 9, the Central Card spot value.

The Quarter values added in the same manner make 5, or the 9 minus the quadrature or 4 in the square.

The Solar values and spirit values have like properties which will be taken up later.

The writer has spent days in study of this Mystic Chart and still finds new wonders upon nearly every examination of it. The combinations of 7 and 9 are truly wonderful, and show the product of a master mind.

We shall again produce it under the head of tarotology and perhaps a third time to illustrate the spirit of numbers and the spirit of potentials in medicine.

All this leads us to an intelligent consideration of the true nature and meaning of the symbolism used in the test book. We find that it consists of a union of the symbols of time, of numbers, of human relations, of spirituality, geometrical forms and astronomy, all within a small compact space without *words* to be misconstrued, misunderstood or mistranslated

We find that everything about these mystic emblems has its particular meaning even to the form in which the spots are arranged.

ASTRONOMICAL ARRANGEMENT.

The 52 emblems or pages represent the 52 weeks in a year.

The 12 court emblems represent the 12 months in a year.

The 13 cards in each suit represent the sun and the 12 signs of the Zodiac.

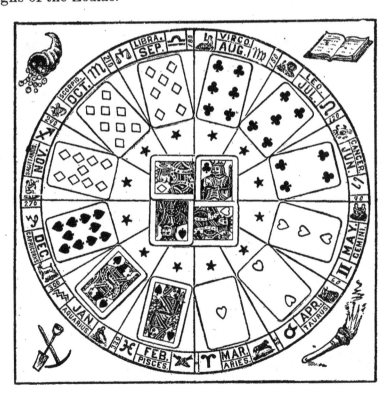

The four suits represent the 4 seasons.

Chart showing the emblems arranged to illustrate the above arrangement will be found on preceding page.

In the spring of the year the birds mate. In the springtime of life or the first quarter, love is the master passion. The heart was therefore chosen as the emblem of the first quarter and the first season. '

The next stage of life is represented by the trefoil or clover leaf of summer. Knowledge is best gained and retained in the summer of life, the second period.

Therefore the shamrock or " club," became the emblem of knowledge, intelligence, heat, argument, or even quarrels and law suits under some planets.

The third season, autumn, has for its emblem the diamond, representative of wealth. The third period of man's life is the one in which he is best able to gain wealth. In the fall of the year the crops are sold and the wealth of the harvest realized.

Winter or the fourth quarter of the Zodiac, is represented by the spade or acorn. By a strange and yet natural transformation, the acorn, which represented the symbolism of the death and burial of the physical form was changed among some nations to the spade which represented the same thing. But the acorn, when planted in the soil, sends forth a life principle which becomes a new tree in time. So it had a deeper signification than the spade, which symbolizes death without resurrection.

But the spade being an instrument of labor, it becomes a symbol of labor and death combined.

In addition to the quadratic division of the test book

there is a two-fold division into dark and light, finally becoming black and red. These symbolize night and day astronomically. The darkness and light of life etc., as applied to man. The 52 emblems being multiplied by the 7 planets under which they rule in succession, make the days in the year, less one. There being no ruling card for the 31st of December.

The Ancient therefore used the 365th day of the year as a holiday, or festival day, doing no work upon that day.

A very few years ago quite a radical change was made in the style of the Court Cards by the manufacturers, by making them "double headers." Before this the Kings and Knaves had legs and feet showing below their Court robes. But the mystic emblems were preserved as far as possible and yet appear as of yore.

The "winged globe" with its seven balls, emblem of mercury, is yet borne by the king of wisdom, and each of his brothers bear secret emblems that have survived the changes of centuries.

Their hair and beards yet curl as in the olden time as they hold up the sword of justice or the battle axe of power.

The Queens look from the same Egyptian eyes, wear the same garb, and hold modestly in their hand the secret lotus flower of innocence and virtue.

The good and industrious queen of spades has not even laid aside her emblem of labor, in all the ages past.

And our good friends, called "Jacks" by some, emblematic of the younger and unmarried portion of the male persuasion, still bear their little emblems. A mystic leaf is seen in the hand of one; but few persons could guess its meaning. They still wear the curled locks. Two being young and two older, the difference can usually be seen upon their faces.

They were originally honest men all, but, being next the Royal Couple, the accceptance of bribes, in modern times, by those in like position, transformed them into "Knaves."

And Knaves they remain to this day.

Now, good friends, some of you may ask, why it is that these characteristics, appertaining to this book and to none other in existence, have been preserved in a world where everything else has changed. Why have not the engravers and printers changed them entirely out of their original form as they have everything else?

Why have they kept them confined to the same number, 52, as of yore?

There could have been no law to compel this wonderful thing.

Why is it then, that, as one authority states, "a pack of cards, substantially the same as those in use now, known to be over a thousand years old, is in existence."

The only anathema ever pronounced against those who should change, by taking away or adding to this book, was promulgated only to the members of the order and has come down to us only as an attachment, fastened upon the end of the mystic book of Revelations, one of the few books written by "inspiration" in the entire Bible.

That could have possessed no terrors, for it has not even protected that ancient work from thousands of changes, interpolations and errors.

Reader, you may well ask these questions. The answer is this: Manufacturers, interested church men and inventors *have* attempted time and time again to change the figures, the emblems, the faces, and even the number of cards in this book. During and after the war of the Rebellion a heavy tax was placed upon cards containing 52 emblems to the pack, or having the well known emblems, hearts, clubs, diamonds and spades upon them.

Manufacturers attempted to change the emblems to certain war emblems, such as crossed swords, cannons, etc; the Court cards were changed to high army officers. One ambitious inventor had beautifully engraved modern kings and queens upon his make of cards Queen Victoria herself appearing as the queen of hearts.

But all in vain. Fortunes were squandered to no purpose. *The people would not have them at any price.* Soldiers would "hang on" to the old, well worn and greasy "test book" and when that could no longer be used, would pay a dollar for a new one, while the gaudy new style cards were cast contemptuously into the ditch by the road-side.

These changes have been attempted in other countries. In Italy and several other Catholic countries, interested parties have thought to do away with this little book, which they call the "devil's picture book," by introducing a highly colored lot of cards with cups and virgins and bells and other devices upon the faces. But you cannot get even an Irishman to use them, and in spite of extensive advertising they have fallen flat.

In the meantime, the manufacturers of the *genuine old magic book,* have grown wealthy and sell at present only in 100 gross lots, to dealers.

They change the backs over and over to every imaginable figure or design. But the faces $must$ remain the same, or they are "no go," as one manufacturer quaintly remarks.

There is no question, whatever, in my mind, but that the magic and mystic symbolism attached to, and connected with the pages of this book, has been the means, the occult means of preserving it intact as shown.

Underneath the physical senses of mankind, there is a psychic recognition of the hidden things in nature. Those who think but very little of such matters, apparently, really recognize the principles of law and the manifestations of the "soul in things." Hard-headed business men, with no spiritual development, that can be discerned, recognize the reign of law, and notice what is called "luck" good and bad. If "luck," so-called, was not a state brought about through regularly acting laws, there could be no constancy to it. Instead of a man's bad luck pursuing him hours, days or weeks at a time, he should be just as likely to have splendid luck one minute after the worst kind.

Although everything in nature exemplifies the law, there is no other thing that illustrates it to such a nicety as does our Magic Test Book.

"Gypsies," those lineal descendants of Egyptian races of olden time, recognize this fact and are noted as "card readers" of human destiny. They have the knowledge through natural descent and intuitive power. But an educated mystic of the order of the Magi can discount the work of the *most expert gypsy* in that line.

Nearly any old card player will tell you wonderful stories of "runs of luck" with cards.

Not one in fifty, who has had any amount of experience with them, will deny the mysterious properties. During my two years experience in the Temple work I have learned that the only persons who do not understand these occult properties, to some extent, even before entering the house of Libra, are those who never handled the cards in their lives and do not even know the names of the emblems. Many such persons quickly discern the occult powers, however, when opportunity offers.

CHAPTER III

An Astronomical Measure.

WHAT IS CHANCE? THE "JOKER" AND ITS VALUE. THE SOLAR YEAR.

CHANCE is defined as accident, or "to happen without assignable cause." For thousands of years men supposed that the elements combined in chance proportions, and they never dreamed that chemistry was an exact science. The stars of heaven were supposed to move about or stand still (?) as "chance" directed. But it is now known that no such thing exists as chance at least in regard to the majority of things, and *we* know that nothing comes by chance.

A true mystic recognizes this at a glance. Those who are not mystics have no use for this book, or the "religion of the stars."

THE JESTER OR JOKER.

A strange fact has been found out by the mystic brotherhood within a few months regarding the "Joker," as it is called.

À few years ago some unknown genius invented it with the object evidently of adding interest to certain games. The first inventor placed all the four quarter emblems, hearts, clubs, diamonds and spades upon the card and made it a universal trump card.

THE KING'S JESTER.

It really "took" but little with the general public, and is usually thrown away. Its presence in a test book will *invalidate every calculation* and render an emblem reading null and void. Emblematically speaking, it seems to be all right, as it was the custom of ancient kings and queens to keep a jester.

In serious affairs this joker counted as nothing, and strange to say, as an astronomical emblem it counted the same. His solar value being zero. But the brotherhood begins to see a hidden meaning to this court fool, after all the "throwing out" he has been subjected to. He represents the *four quarters* by virtue of his four suits and the center or place of kings by his court value, making what is called the five points. This really represents five quarters, in number symbolism.

If such should be a fact, the test book would represent the entire motion of the earth about the sun, or the astronomical year, 52 weeks, plus one and one-fourth days. Then from another standpoint, which seems to bear out the view already taken, we have the reckoning of the spot values of all the cards as follows:

The four Kings 4x13 - - -	=	52
" " Queens 4x12	=	48
" " Knaves 4x11 - - -	=	44
" " Tens 4x10 - - -	=	40
" " Nines 4x9	—	36
32 other spot cards	=	144
The Joker - - -	=	$1\frac{1}{4}$
Total	=	$365\frac{1}{4}$

Exactly the days in a solar year.

If this is "chance" as remarked by the immortal Kepler, "it comes so near a law as to set one thinking." Again, we have the rulings of each card under each of the planets; 7 times 52, plus 5 quarters making up the year complete.

We have now considered the various properties of the test book, and before proceeding to deeper studies will simply explain that the word "test," means to prove, measure, weigh and try.

All dictionaries agree in saying that the word "test" comes from the root "taste," and the reader is requested to observe how occultly the writer of Revelations brings out the fact that he alluded to the " little book" when he speaks of the " taste " being "sweet as honey "

Looked at from the ordinary point of view, it is absurd to speak of "tasting" a book, but when we understand that the Mystic Brother "tested" it when he "devoured " it, as so many others have done since then, we see the very beautiful manner in which he concealed his language.

The Bible is full of these sealed messages, which can only be read by the initiated.

The word "testament" was taken from this same root, and the Christian regards his new testament as a tester of the truth.

Candid reader, which book has the best right to the name?

In my humble opinion the answer is an easy one to give.

ASTRAL NUMBERS OF THINGS.

Everything that exists, large or small, possesses a number that exactly gives a mathematical expression of the thing itself.

If the constitution of the thing is complex, the number is complex.

If it be simple in constitution, the astral number is simple.

AS AN ILLUSTRATION.

Oxygen has for its number -	1030
Hydrogen has for its number -	212
Nitrogen has for its number	1969
Carbon has for its number - - -	1050

These numbers are nearly simples, except that the combining force numbers are included.

Water is a compound of hydrogen 2 equations, oxygen

one. Its number is 1010, being *less even than one of its constituents*. This is caused through the suppression of the combining force numbers.

Of course, a general treatment of this branch of the subject is out of place here, as it will require a large book to treat astro-chemistry alone, as it requires.

Not only physical things have these numbers, but abstracts, such as certain dates or periods of time have their expressions in numbers.

Thus we have the nativity numbers, the environment numbers, and the astral numbers of persons.

These numbers are useful in many mathematical calculations in the occult line.

The writer's nativity number is 644699; a very peculiar one, by the way, as will be seen upon close examination.

THE SPIRIT OF NUMBERS.

Every number, however large, has its spirit or occult root, which brings the expression of the number down to certain bounds, within the powers of expression in tables and books.

If the number of the physical is small, the spirit may be much larger than the number.

The spirit numbers may be taken on a high scale and so consist of several figures, but the one used by the Brotherhood of Magic is the one found by means of the number 9, called the Nth root by some.

The spirit root of a number is equal to the Nth root of one-ninth of the number, plus ten times the enumerator of any fraction that may arise from the division of the number by nine.

To obtain this spirit by an easy method, simply divide the number by nine, reduce the quotient to the Nth root and place the remainder, if any, to the left of it.

Example. What is the spirit root of 1844? Ans. 86.

Found as follows:

$$9)1844(204=6$$
$$\underline{18}$$
$$44$$
$$\underline{36}$$
$$86$$

The Nth root is found by adding the figures composing a number together, continuously until but one figure remains.

The Nth root has by itself many wonderful qualities, which I may speak of and illustrate further, before this work is ended.

SPIRITS AND NUMBERS OF THE MYSTIC EMBLEMS.

Like everything else the "Mystic Test Book" has its number, its spirit root and its environment number. Not only this, but each card has its individual number, spirit and environment. Each card has its solar value which is constant, like the astral number of a person.

The spirit number or root of a card is obtained from the solar value; so the spirit is a constant. But all other values, spirits and numbers change all the time as the earth changes its polarity.

Emblems change values from day to day, from hour to hour, from minute to minute, and one value changes every five seconds.

THE EMBLEM VALUE OF CARDS.

Hearts=0   Clubs=13   Diamonds=26   Spades=39.

These values are called "suit values."

The "quarter values" of the same are:

$$1 \; : \; 2 \; : \; 3 \; : \; 4$$

The "spot values" are the numbers of the spots on each card.

But, Knaves count as 11, Queens as 12 and Kings as 13.

These spot values added together for the whole test book=364. This is equal to the cards in the book multiplied by the 7 planets.

7 times 52=364. Add the "Joker" or "Jester" which represents the four quarters and the sun, and is equal to five-fourths, and we get $365\frac{1}{4}$, the days in a year.

It is a remarkable fact that on the 31st of December the Jester rules supreme, even the "Members of the Court" bow to him.

When we take out 52 weeks from our year, we have the same "day" left on our hands.

THE SOLAR VALUE OF THE CARDS

is found by adding the spot value to the suit value.

The spirit root of this solar value is the "spirit of the emblem."

TAKE FOR EXAMPLE THE FOLLOWING CARDS:

Spot value 5	8	12	10	4
Suit value 0	26	13	39	26
Solar value 5	34	25	49	30
Spirit value 50	73	72	45	33

Observe how *very different the spirits are from the other values,* as I have some strange facts to present in relation to this later on.

SYMBOLISM OF THE SUITS.

Now, each emblem in the Mystic Test Book has a nature, or characteristic, corresponding to one of the planets in both the suit and spots.

Venus and Mercury rule hearts.

Mars and Earth rule clubs.

Jupiter and Neptune rule diamonds.

Saturn and Uranus rule spades.

But these couplets of planets do not give the same characteristic to the same emblem.

While Venus rules an emblem from a point of friendship and love, Mercury rules it from a point of passion.

Mars rules clubs mainly from the point of lawsuits, quarrels and heat; while Terra rules in clubs from the standpoint of knowledge

Jupiter cards, diamonds, indicate wealth.

Neptune cards, diamonds, indicate commerce.

Saturn cards, spades, from a standpoint of death.

Uranus cards, spades, from a point of labor.

GEOMETRICAL SYMBOLISM.

We have briefly glanced at the symbolism of the suits, or spot emblems and the numbers in the foregoing remarks. We will now consider the occult meanings of the geometrical form of the single cards and co-ordinates. The co-ordinate of any card in spot value is one containing an equal number of spots. The co-ordinate card in spirit, is one having a spirit value equal to the solar value of the other. The following couplets are co-ordinate in spirit and solar values.

Solar value card leading in each couple.

The first two being *double co-ordinates,* the only such in the Test Book. Co-ordinates in spirit and suit are common; the second couplet being an example.

ILLUSTRATION OF GEOMETRIC SYMBOLISM.

Emblems of Monotony.　　*Trouble.　Change.*

This row of cards represent a personal " path of life."

By laying out the actual emblems from the Test Book as represented here, cne can observe the symbolism to better advantage.

The sixes show a life, for a time, moving in straight lines, with nothing out of the usual routine. But at the fourth card an obstacle comes in the way, trouble comes. The five shows a change, as it represents a cross, **X**, in one's path; the lines change in one's life and a journey perhaps removes the person from the preceding monotony

These are the general characteristics of those cards, the variations coming from the planets they rule under at the time

The twos indicate unions or joinings; bargains between two persons. Co-partnership and letters passing from person to person.

Threes indicate indecision, or a place where two ways open before one, as if the spot in the center was the person

ILLUSTRATION OF UNIONS AND INDECISIONS.

and the other spots the two ways leading in two directions.

POWER, DEVELOPEMENT AND SUCCESS.

This entire row represents symmetrical fullness or rounding out, just as the spots are arranged on the emblems.

The eights indicate power to overcome obstacles, spiritual advancement and numbers of persons, congregations or gatherings of people.

The tens represent success, as if one stood in the open space between the spots, surrounded with success upon all sides.

The geometrical form on the nines is a representation of a path with a disappointing obstacle in the center. Approach from either end and it bars your progress. You are disappointed and turned back.

The seven is a trouble, from *one way* only. Approach it from another direction and trouble disappears.

By these few illustrations, which should be carefully studied by the student of card delineation, we have shown that the geometrical forms have a meaning of their own.

THE COURT OF DISAPPOINTMENT AND TROUBLE.

Some of our students have been at a loss to understand how it could be, that seven, a sacred number representing spirit, should indicate trouble. The explanation is this: The spiritual and material are, as one might say, antipodes of each other. Sevens do *not* indicate spiritual trouble, but material. Some of the most advanced persons, in a spiritual way, have the most trouble from material surroundings and environments, being antagonistic to their natures. This is a natural law, and I can advise all, from my own experience, that, if they wish to become rich in this world's goods, they had better let their spiritual nature remain undeveloped and dwarfed. A "mystic" lays up his treasure in heaven and not upon earth.

He deals in coin that can be taken out with him into the grander life beyond the grave, and he knows full well that "shrouds have no pockets"

THE TEST BOOK IN ITS RELATIONS TO TIME AND MAGNETIC FORCES.

The first form of the Test Book is known as the "solar"

book or the natural order book. In this book each emblem occupies a place corresponding to its own value.

TO FORM A NATURAL TEST BOOK.

Pile the first quarter cards, hearts, face up from ace to king. Do the same with the 2nd, 3rd and 4th quarter emblems, ending with king of spades. The emblems are now in the natural order according to the Zodiac.

RULING EMBLEMS

In every pack of cards, no matter how much or by whom shuffled, mixed or cut, there are seven cards that rule under the seven planets. These rulers change in accordance with the occult principles of time and the magnetism of the person or persons handling them.

There are several ways of finding these ruling emblems by mathematical process and psychic powers, but the most ready means is to find them by the following easy mechanical process.

When the book is fully prepared by any process required, begin at the top of the book, which is *always the back of the cards* and deal them into 7 piles one by one, finishing each pile as you go. Begin at Mercury.

| Mer. | Ven. | Mars | Jup. | Sat. | Ura. | Nep. |

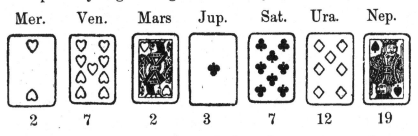

| 2 | 7 | 2 | 3 | 7 | 12 | 19 |

The figures under each card show how many cards are to be placed in that pile.

The cards given are the rulers in a natural order, or solar

book. The cards on top of each pile are represented as turned over face up.

Lay off each ruling card to the right of the pile; place the pile on top of it and pile them all on Neptune pile in regular order from Uranus to Mercury.

Now quadrate the book as per instructions given else-where, and as many times as you please, and you will find that unless the book is shuffled or cut, these rulers always come under the seven planets when spread again. *Not always the same planets,* but they are all there.

By an examination of the cards in each pile you will find that every card, other than these 7 rulers, have been scattered to the "four winds of heaven," symbolically speaking, by the quadration. Make 2 quadrates and each of these rulers rules under same planet as in a solar book.

By keeping up the quadrating until you have covered the degree in one quarter of the Zodiac, that is 90 quadrates, you will find every emblem in its original solar place.

So far, we have only the results of pure mathematical principles; but the moment we introduce *personal magnetism* and the actions of individuals under the astral forces prevail-ing at the time, we have new elements which must be taken into consideration.

Let a person "cut" the Test Book, which is performed by taking a portion of the book off from the top, placing it upon the table and placing the remaining part upon it, and a change takes place along the whole line, with a new set of emblems in the ruling places

Let a person shuffle or mix the cards up for a period of 60 seconds and the place of every emblem corresponds to his personal magnetism. Let him cut the book so prepared, 3 times in succession, with just 20 seconds interval between, and the ruling places are occupied by the cards ruling at the time, under the seven planets.

Now, quadrate the book and lay it out in the grand spread and *every card in the Test Book* comes under the planet where it rules with that person at the time, past, present or future, according to whether the planetary effect represented by it is at maximum, waxing or waning.

The lay outs or "grand spreads" in this book are illustrations of actual quadrates from time shuffles and cuts, in regular order on selected minutes. They are nearly all from mv own magnetism; as it is necessary to have a set all by one person, of at least 52 lay outs in order to make a study of the subject.

At first sight any lay out seems to have no particular plan or form, illustrating the action of fixed laws. But the more you study these lay outs the greater will your wonder be at the evidences of an *occult force* back of the emblems.

Examine the spreads in this book and compare them one by one, and you will soon begin to observe the peculiar movements of certain ruling cards of co-ordinate values in spirit and solar values, as well as spots.

Then shuffle a book, cut it as instructed, quadrate it, spread it as hereinafter taught and observe the same evidences of law with yourself. Notice the peculiar grouping of the colors. The light and dark shades in your life, the couplets of co-ordinating emblems, et.c, etc. You will soon begin to see that there is a "spirit behind the cards" that can and does make itself manifest.

The quadrations used as illustrations in this work are made at certain selected hours, minutes and seconds and then assorted according to the magnetic effects.

No other person would produce spreads exactly like these, but the general effect is the same and from these spreads calculations and prognostications can be made for any person or persons.

One spread is given for the culmination of each minute, with the sun card progressing according to the solar values.

The following plate shows the arrangement of a grand spread with particular reference to the planetary rulings and the lines denoting the three periods of time, past, present and future. The two perpendicular lines upon the right and part of the third denoting the past. The center line and part of each line to the right and left of it belongs in the present effect, which covers a few days of time, or the effect of the present aspect upon the person. The rows of hearts and clubs, and part of the diamond row refer to the future. This layout is not a quadrate, being simply arranged to show the first 7 spot value cards under the planets of same number, in order to familiarise the student with the number and rotation of the planets. Upon the right the cards are partly arranged in a form to indicate the planets they each rule under the strongest. Thus the kings are under Jupiter denoting power and rule.

Tens under Uranus denoting success. Nines under Saturn indicating disappointment.

Queens under Venus the female planet and ruler of love. Of course this is all from a symbolical point of view only.

PRESENT.

★ ★ ★ ★   ★ ★ ★ ★

FUTURE.   PAST.

PLANETARY, LIFE AND TIME LINES OF GRAND SPREAD.

Perpendicular rows are life lines; horizontal, planetary; top line, sun cards; the middle one being the solar time card.

The student is advised though, to make a study of this plate in order to become perfectly familiar with the planetary lines and other items mentioned. The suits upon the right indicate the characteristic suits of the planets at the other end of the horizontal lines, an explanation of which has been heretofore given.

DIRECTIONS FOR PREPARING THE TEST BOOK.

The person who is to receive the reading we will call C. The one who is to give the reading we will call B.

1st. C thoroughly shuffles and mixes the cards, in any way most natural to him, for just *one minute*; B holding a watch and keeping the time, which should be started on an even minute if possible.

2nd. At the end of one minute C places the book upon the sun and cuts it once *immediately*. The cut is performed by taking off a portion of the emblems, laying them upon the cloth and placing the balance of the book thereon.

3rd. At just 20 seconds later C is directed by B to cut again, which must be done exactly on time to secure correct results. At the end of 20 seconds more C cuts for the third and last time. The book is now ready for

THE PLANETARY CUTTING.

Although a reading *can* be given upon an ordinary table, experts always use a Zodiac table cloth, when one is obtainable. When the Zodiac is not used, the piles of cards are laid about the table in as near a circle about the central pile as is convenient.

4th. C cuts a few cards from the top of the center or sun pile and places them in the house of the Zodiac corresponding to his month of birth. If no Zodiac is used C must fix a point on the table as his birth month

5th. He then cuts off some more cards and places them in any house he feels impressed to put them in.

6th. C repeats this operation until he has 7 piles around the circle, the last pile consuming the last of the sun cards. If the cards in the sun pile run out before the seven piles are completed, C must cut some off from the pile already in the circle to make up the number.

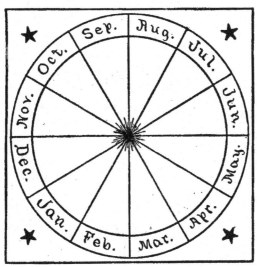

THE ZODIAC TABLE CLOTH USED IN READINGS.

There must always be a distinct pile of two or more cards for each of the seven planets, or the results are worthless.

DRAWING THE RULING EMBLEMS. MARRIED MALES.

7th. C must now begin at the pile of cards nearest to Aries, or the first pile to the right of the lower Celestial Meridian, select one card from the pile, make a record of it upon a paper or tablet and place the card face down upon the sun. He then passes on in the direction the months run and does the same for each pile in succession, until he has seven cards piled upon the sun.

8th. If the person is unmarried, he must begin at exactly the opposite polarity, or the house of Libra, September, and proceed as directed in section 7.

EXCEPTIONS TO THIS ORDER.

Females, if single, should begin at Virgo, or August, and draw in retrograde to the months. Married females should begin at Pisces, February, and draw in retrograde order, but in all other respects in the same manner as set forth in section 7.

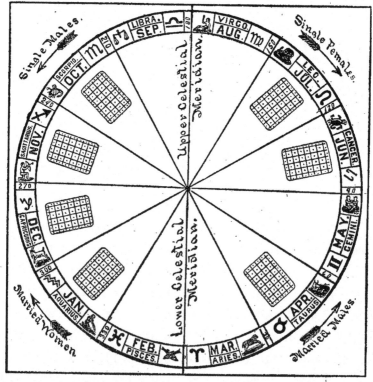

CUT SHOWING ZODIAC HOUSES AND MONTHS, WITH PILE OF CARDS AS PLACED.

9th. In case the Zodiac cloth is not used, the draw must start from any pile C feels impressed to start with. If the personal intuition is strong, the results will be excellent, but with persons of low intuitive powers I would emphatically recommend the Zodiac, if it is nothing more than a sheet of white paper marked off with a pencil like the illustration shown above.

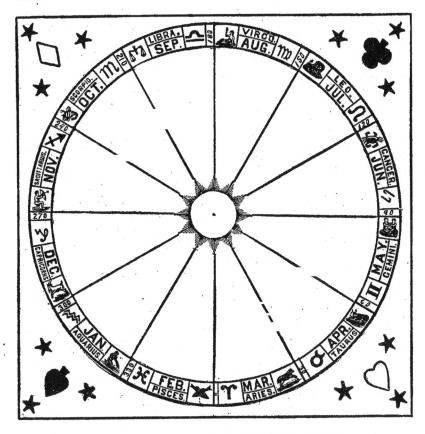

THE WALL ZODIAC OR TRESTLE-BOARD.

For actual use, the signs and figures other than the months and names of houses may be omitted. Our Chicago mystics use a table cloth of blue broadcloth embroidered with yellow silk, and most of them have in addition, a wall trestle-board where the movable planets are kept set up to their exact place from day to day, as in the Grand Temple

Those who make an exact science of this art, are thus enabled to better determine the effect of a given combination of cards under certain planets, by knowing exactly where those planets are at the time. But our aim is to make this book useful to others besides those versed in astrological and astronomical science; so we say that all these accessories, although useful to the expert, can be dispensed with by the amateur astral card reader.

PILING THE EMBLEMS.

10th. When the 7 planetary ruling cards are drawn and recorded by C, as heretofore directed, he must take them from the sun, or center, and place them upon the pile of cards in the house or division of the Zodiac containing his *birth month.* He then lifts that entire pile and places it upon another, where he feels impressed to place it. He continues this until all the cards are in one pile (always faces down) which he places upon the sun.

11th. B now holds the time and directs C to cut the book at the *exact beginning of a minute* and it makes no difference what minute of the hour it is, except that if the first cutting was on an *even minute of time* by the time piece used, this second cutting must be on an even minute by the same time piece. If the watch keeps correct seconds and minutes it makes no difference whether it is minutes or hours out of the way on standard or solar time. If the first cut, that is the cut in preparing the packs as directed in section 2, is *started at an odd minute* the one mentioned herein must be on an *odd one.*

12th. C cuts three times at intervals of *ten seconds,* just half the time interval used before. If B feels impressed to ask C to shuffle the book before this last triple cut he should inform C; in which case C should take the book entirely up from the table and shuffle it *in hand* until B gives the time to start the cutting as per section eleven.

You may not think all this care is important; but I assure you that it is. No matter whether you understand *why it is or not.* The time elements and the triplex cut corresponding to the first or triplex deal of the quadrature are of the greatest value, and a careful observance of these small particulars has been the basis of the writer's success in the occult demonstrations with the Mystic Test Book. I have heard a careless student remark "what is 10 or 15 seconds, that they should amount to anything ?" Do you know, friends, how far this ball we live upon has moved in that little time of 15 seconds ? It has moved ahead more than *two hundred and twenty-five miles* in its orbit and has, at the same time, changed its polar angle accordingly, relative to the sun. Its axial rotation at the equator has been about four miles during that little insignificant quarter of a minute. But we are now ready for the next step.

QUADRATION OF THE TEST BOOK.

13th. B takes the book in hand and removes the three top cards, without disturbing the order in which they come, and places them in the first or heart quarter of the Zodiac. The next three he places in the same manner in the club quarter, then three in the diamond and three in the spade quarter, and so on, until all but four cards are piled in the quarters. These four cards are to be placed singly around the four quarters.

EXPLANATION OF THIS DEAL.

The three cards to each quarter, at the four first rounds, are emblematic of the three houses in each quarter of the Celestial Circle. Three times four making twelve, the months in a year and the number of cards in each pile before the last four are placed thereon. When the deal is finished there are thirteen cards in each quarter; the thirteen being the figure of knowledge and equal to the parts of the Zodiac, namely the twelve houses and the sun or center.

THE SINGLE QUADRATE.

14th. B now piles the cards upon the first quarter, or heart quarter, in the order of the months and signs and makes a deal of one card at a time from the top of the book around and around the Zodiac from the first quarter until he has thirteen cards again piled in each quarter Of course, the deal must end at the spade quarter, or it shows an error in the deal in some manner.

15th. Gather the emblems on to the heart quarter pile, and have them cut twice, five seconds apart.

LAYING THE GRAND SPREAD.

16th. To perform this work, B takes the book in hand and begins at the top and lays off the cards one by one, face up, beginning at the right hand end of the table, one card space from that end, until he has laid seven cards; when he begins again at the side nearest himself and starts the next row and proceeds thus until he has laid off 7 rows, one for each of the 7 planets.

He then deals the next card to the right hand end opposite the 3d perpendicular row, the next beyond it and next beyond that, thus ending the spread. This last short row are the "sun cards" so called, because they do not rule under any of the planets.

On a succeeding page will be found a quadratic grand spread from a "natural order," or what is called Solar Test Book. Pile the cards from the ace of hearts to the king of spades, face up, turn the book over and quadrate it as heretofore directed. Spread it as instructed in the preceding sections and the lay-out will present the aspect shown in illustration.

This is what is called an "independent solar spread," and is devoid of personal or magnetic qualities and wholly arbitrary in formation. But the quadrate has thrown the emblems into their respective planetary places, relative to abstract position, in the same manner as if the formation was a magnetic one. So it is worthy of study.

The grand spread is now ready for reading and delineating.

This is the most important part of all, and I wish to say right here before going any farther, that any person who expects or supposes that he or she can master the intricate art of emblem delineation in a few hours, a few days or even in a few months, may as well change his or her mind upon the subject at once.

Such is the infinite variety of the combinations and

The Mystic Test Book.

interpretations constantly coming up, that great judgment and intuitive powers are needed to give the correct meanings. In the lay-outs and tables of definitions used in this work, I have taken the utmost pains to make them clear and easily understood, but I constantly realize from letters received daily that a large number of people *do not try to understand*. They seem to *hate to think*, and therefore ask a hundred questions regarding matters that are before them in print. I have had dozens, yes hundreds of letters covering page after page of manuscript, written by people who admit that they have "Temple Lectures, or the Religion of the Stars," and our O. O. M. paper, as well as bulletins, yet they ask "are ladies admitted?" "Do you believe in evolution?" "How came you to get into this work?" and so on *ad infinitum*. Some good souls sit down and pour out 25 to 35 pages of foolscap manuscript giving their private views on such subjects as re-incarnation, evolution of the soul, astral magnetism and so on through all the subjects treated upon by me in my lectures.

Now, my dear good friends, while I appreciate the kind feelings that actuate most of you in this, I beg you to remember that I am a very busy man, my time is exceedingly valuable, compared with most people's, and furthermore, that your *private views* are useless to me. What I have to say is in print. Read it, digest it, and make as much or as little of it as you are able. It matters not whether you like it or hate it, if you have any views upon the subjects treated, give them to the world in print. I assure you that if they are worth considering, editors will gladly print them.

Pray excuse this digression, my friends; I do not complain or want to complain, and I acknowledge the receipt of thousands of such good, kind and appreciative letters as would expand the heart of any one. But I foresee that the publication of this book will bring forth a host of questions unless I warn the public that I cannot answer them personally. If I find that some particular points are not generally understood, and it is possible to elucidate them more perfectly, I shall issue a printed bulletin containing the explanations.

Before going on with the directions for reading, it will be well perhaps to give instructions for finding the card of day and the birth card, for these cards frequently have an important bearing upon the delineations of the astral spread. The mode of finding the day card or birth card is precisely the same, for the day card ruling upon any particular date is the birth card of any person born at that time. This card has a part to play all through the life, as it is, as one might say, a type or emblem of the effects of the magnetism of the earth and planets at the time of the person's birth. What the signs and letters X, Y and Z are to algebra, the symbols composing the Mystic Test Book are to our astral calculations.

We "test" our work at every point. The writer discovered the error in the tables of Herschel and other astronomers, as to the motion of Jupiter, through the failure of the accepted tables to bring that planet to the point where his magnetic effect would correspond to that found by actual trial with the Test Book in 1887. The tables of motion of each planet were then tested separately before being used in our books, as an error in such expensive works would have been serious indeed. The other planetary tables of motion were correct. We have in this Grand Temple a set of tables that are so correct, that one hundred years motion of any planet, carried back by the law of multiple cycles, will not vary *one second of arc* in all that long period. There are only two sets of such tables in existence and they cost almost an infinite amount of labor to calculate and record.

Upon page 63 will be found a plate, showing the ruling cards of time. In the left hand column are a row of figures indicating the tens, while the top row indicates the units of the numbers composing the spirit of the powers used.

The following tables give the numerical powers of the planets according to the latest data. They differ slightly from the tables published by Lillie, being as correct as human intelligence can make them.

ASTRAL POWERS OF THE MONTHS.

Jan., 161623	Jul., 491281
Feb., 266435	Aug., 324824
Mar., 334149	Sep., 353658
Apr., 498658	Oct., 227944
May, 597719	Nov., 217412
Jun., 693378	Dec., 188169

RULE FOR FINDING DAY OR BIRTH CARDS.

This is a very simple mathematical operation.

Take, the astral power of the month.

The astral power of the day.

Add them together.

Find the spirit of the sum, which indicates in the table, the card ruling.

EXAMPLE FOR PRACTICE.

Find what card rules on the 23d day of July.

Astral power for July	491281
Astral power for 23d	386139
	877420

The spirit of this last number is 13. See directions for finding spirits of numbers.

This indicates row No. 1, 3d card from the left in the plate of day cards, which is the five of clubs. This is only one of many rules for finding emblems of various divisions of time.

ASTRAL POWERS OF THE DAYS.

1,	157741	12,	622346	23,	386139
2,	213144	13,	491125	24,	408758
3,	256883	14,	361848	25,	683569
4,	358942	15,	236459	26,	524160
5,	461973	16,	186886	27,	362807
6,	533819	17,	169389	28,	269494
7,	616519	18,	154727	29,	246165
8,	656370	19,	221875	30,	198536
9,	722465	20,	233538	31,	163543
10,	881872	21,	274361		
11,	719547	22,	376420		

POSITION OF THE BIRTH CARD.

In a grand spread, from one person's magnetism, that person's birth card occupies a position in the spread where the *strongest* and *nearest effects concentrate*. Therefore the emblem reader should notice particularly the position of the birth card, and, for the purpose of avoiding error, it is well in practice, to lay a counter or a small piece of money upon that card to designate it.

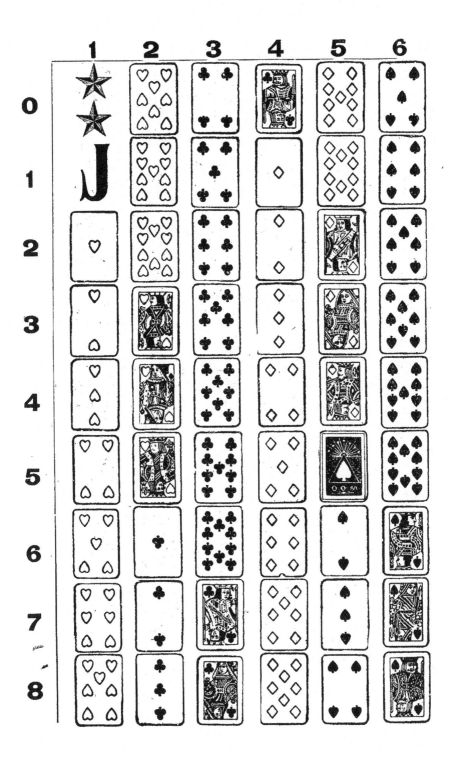

If this card is in the past, it shows that the indications around it for a distance of 2 cards, point to something recent. If in the future part of the spread, it shows something to come soon. But the indications so shown near the birth card apply *personally*, while the *general* indications point to the usual events and to other person's lives connected with C's, just the same as if C's birth card was not in that quarter. So emblems frequently *indicate doubly*, showing events long past and those near at hand simultaneously, as well as those far in the future, co-ordinating with the present.

When the birth card comes in the exact center of the lay-out, where the "sun line" crosses the line of Jupiter, it is an excellent indication and shows that the planetary influences are well in balance and predicts good fortune. But the nature of this good fortune depends upon the nature of the birth card. If this is a "power card" it indicates well-balanced strength and power. If it is a nine, it shows that C will overcome his disappointment.

Approximate positions to center of lay-out are proportionately fortunate.

THE MYSTIC CROSS.

This is considered an important factor, and indicates some hidden thing in C's life. But the nature depends upon the direction of the cross and whether the greater portion comes under Saturn or the minor planets, Mars, Mercury and Venus.

THE HORIZONTAL CROSS OF MARS.

This cross is shown in face cards in order to make

it more conspicuous, and crosses of all kinds are usually nearly all in court cards. But they frequently occur in colors.

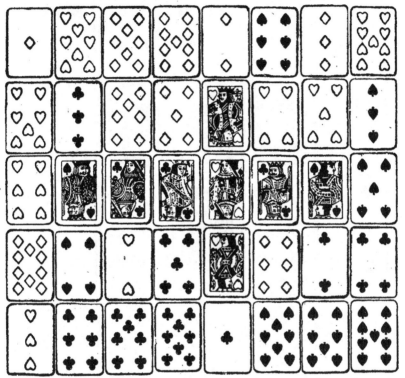

For instance, the cross may be all in red cards completely surrounded by black ones, or *vice versa*. Once last year a lady had an " *eight emblem* " cross *all in hearts*, come with its upright under Saturn. Of course, this was very exceptional. When I delineated it to her she burst into tears and admitted the cross was only *too* true in its signification.

Crosses may occur in all sorts of positions with indications according to the planets in the cross. There may be more or less cards in the cross.

EXAMPLES OF MYSTIC CROSSES.

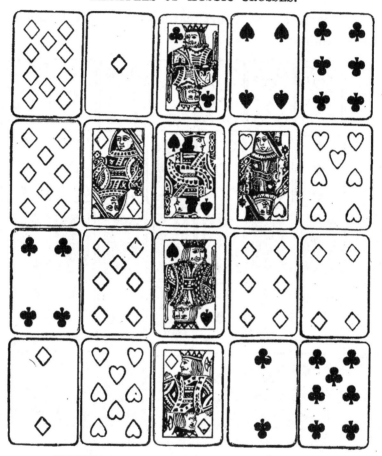

PERPENDICULAR CROSS IN COURT CARDS.

The reason these forms are called " Mystic " Crosses, is because they show evidences of "mind force" back of the work. An intellectuality present. That is, that some outside power, acting *within the law,* however, is present and acting upon the person.

As a scientist, upon investigating these mysterious forces some two or three years ago, suggested that this peculiarity *might* be accounted for under the so-called " laws of chance," we, together, made elaborate calculations, to find, if possible, that such was the case. We made seven grand spreads within twelve hours, strictly on time, and found three crosses, two solid squares and a perfect triangle in court cards, besides a number of minor mystic combinations.

PERPENDICULAR CROSS IN HEARTS.

We then calculated that the chances upon such a series of events transpiring in a "world of chance," were about one to 375,000,000. So a person might spread lay-outs all his life long, day and night, without a ghost of a chance to make such manifestations of law. But our proof of the action of law and intellectuality combined, upon everything in nature, including the Mystic Test Book, does not rest upon such evidence as this alone, fortunately.

The sample spreads in this work are purposely freed from mystic symbols, being simply the result of time and planetary laws.

HORIZONTAL GREEK CROSS IN COURT CARDS.

The reason for this is, that the emblems have general positions at certain times, called culminations, which apply to the general characteristics of all persons. That is, the emblems ruling with B at a certain time in certain given positions, will rule with C at another certain time. There is but one way to find which spread in this work gives this general position, and that is, by finding what spread has a ruling sun card, the same as the one in the spread under consideration occupying the *same position*. This position is directly under the sun in the short row at the top.

RULE FOR FINDING THE LAY-OUT.

Take the sun card in table spread.

Set down the suit value. Put under it the spot value.

Put under this the number 7.

Add all together. Multiply the sum by 2.

Add to the product, the number 61.

This gives the page of the book where that sun card rules under the sun.

In the grand spread thus found, the emblems are in their normal position relative to their planetary effects at the time. You can then readily determine by a comparison with the table spread, where the variations from the normal are greater or less. For instance; suppose the normal position of the ten of diamonds, under the ruling, is under Jupiter. But, in the table spread it is under Saturn. You can then confidently predict that a pecuniary success which *should* come to the person under the normal effects of the planets has been counteracted by environments.

Ordinary emblem readers do not usually go into these finer calculations, being guided a great deal by intuition, but I wish to give these directions for the benefit of students who wish to make a deep study of the subject.

When the spread is completed, it is usual to designate the planetary cards drawn by the person, by turning them at right angles to their former positions.

CUT SHOWING TURNED CARDS.

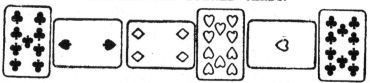

The 9 c, 10 h and 10 c being the drawn cards. The pair of tens with an ace between constitute a pair of "mystic bars," as they are called. They are quite often seen in spreads and have occult meanings in accordance with the characteristics of the cards forming the bars. The cards thus turned in the spread are called "significators," as they are significant of many things. In the first place they are double in power to what they would be if not drawn cards. Secondly, they affect the combinations connected with them in immediate contact.

GENERAL LINES OF DARKNESS AND LIGHT.

Independent of the individual definitions of the cards, the reader should look particularly after the lines of light and dark as they have a particular signification apart from the suits or spot values. The dark cards indicate the darkness in one's life. The red cards (originally white, in ancient times) indicate the light or happy portions. In some lives you will trace these lines of red diagonally across from Mercury in the past, up to Neptune in the future. When this is the case, it indicates that C *did*, for many years, find his happiness under the planets of love and passion. Later, military and pecuniary feelings swayed him, or perhaps athletic exercises, boating, fishing, etc., as Mars rules matters appertaining to power and strength in the physical.

Later, he has his pleasure in spiritual unfoldment and soul culture.

If it reaches into Neptune, he will take great delight in travel and sight seeing. Dark bands covering diagonal lines reaching through the life lines (perpendicular lines) indicate an antagonistic influence running all through C's life.

Isolated patches of dark or light, cut off entirely from all emblems of the same color, are very interesting.

A remarkable case of this kind came up in a reading given to a stranger in 1891, by the author. It was so remarkable that I made a record of the part containing the "island of light" as I term such positions.

THE ISLAND OF LIGHT.

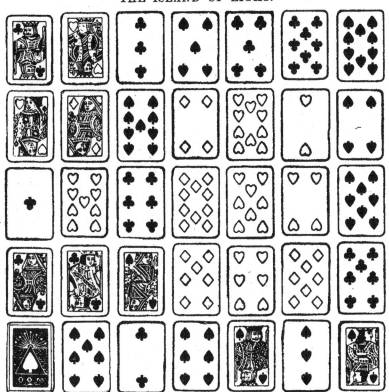

I delineated it as a beautiful, happy, successful and contented spot in his past life, that was preceded and surrounded upon all sides by darkness, trouble and disappointment. But the 4 d and 7 d reaching up to the middle or present life line indicated that this bright spot in his life was just drawing to a close.

When I had finished the delineation, the gentleman quietly explained how exactly the emblems had illustrated his life. The student is advised, to look particularly for these little points and indicators, as they afford much information regarding the person's life and surroundings.

For the purpose of convenience, the tables of indications in this work are placed opposite the plate containing the grand spread, where the card defined rules as a sun card.

If the student will learn thoroughly the way in which the solar natural book runs, he can very soon find the page con taining the definitions of any particular card wanted without reference to the page or rule for finding same. The rule is given, only because other spreads are in the book with same cards under the sun. But the defining tables are just 52 in number and consecutively arranged. The suits run—

HEARTS: CLUBS: DIAMONDS: SPADES.

The spots under each suit run in regular order from ace to king.

The definitions given are not intended to be inflexibly correct or unchangeable. Such is the almost infinite number of combinations of the 52 emblems, that it is impossible to foresee and record all the various meanings. Besides this, the delineator must bear in mind that the personal environment of the person represented in the spread has much to do with meanings of the emblems. For instance; a 9 of diamonds following a seven under Saturn, or with a 7 of diamonds under Jupiter in the same life line, indicates for a rich man a loss of a large sum of money, but a poor man with the same proportionate "ill luck," so-called, might only lose a few dollars. In the same manner, the environment of marriage makes an immense difference in the meanings of the emblems. Where the 2h followed by the 8h and 4h under Venus, indicates an engagement and marriage for single persons, it indicates spiritual advancement, union of forces, contentment of heart and soul, for the married.

It is confidently asserted by the Mystic Brotherhood, that no single "environment" exists, that so completely changes the magnetic respondences of individuals as that of marriage.

This is the secret of why it is, that some people are changed for the better and some for the worse by this union. Perhaps the very planetary influences that were favorable to you when single became adverse as soon as you were united to another being.

I believe the time will come, when these forces will be taken into consideration *before* marriage, instead of *after*, and many unhappy alliances obviated thereby.

Before going on with the tables of indications I wish to say a few words regarding the time and manner of giving or receiving emblem readings.

First. *No person should ever attempt more than one spread in the same day.* There are certain magnetic forces used in the full work, which become changed or exhausted so that a second spread for that person will give, but partial results. That is, always providing that the first one given is correctly carried through. I do not mean by this, that no person should delineate for *others,* more than once, but, that he should not attempt to read for *himself* but once in a day. Some persons are so constituted that once a week is fully often enough.

Second. The manner of going about it. One who wishes correct results, should go about the preparation of the book in the same careful, painstaking, and as one might almost say "devout"frame of mind that the churchman experiences when opening the book *he* regards as sacred. I have noticed that occult emblems very rarely have anything to give to the idle and curious seekers after sensations.

The power back of the *Mystic Test Book* knows well the meaning of the expression once used by a teacher in olden time, relative to "pearls" and certain domestic animals.

It is not expected that every owner of this book will become an expert card reader ; any more than that every initiate of the Grand Temple will become an astrologer and astronomer. Some can comprehend but little at the best. Some will think that a hurried glance at these pages, in the intervals of business, ought to give them the knowledge they seek, or else the whole thing is a humbug. But all such will fail to get what they seek; and it cannot be helped. Those who seek for light and wish to know the secret and order of the universe, must make a regular and careful study as far as their other duties will permit, or they will accomplish but little.

We shall now proceed to give the lay-outs and card definitions, leaving the other matters to come after.

In order, however, that the student may have the entire directions summarized within a small compass I will give here a review.

A RECAPITULATION OF WORK.

1. Arrangement of cloth upon table.
2. Tablet and pencil for recording cards.
3. C shuffles the book one minute.
4. B keeping account of the time.
5. C cuts 3 times at intervals of 20 seconds, starting on any even minute selected by B.
6. , C cuts the book into 7 piles, as more fully explained in former sections.
7. C selects one card from each pile under rules given heretofore.
8. C makes a careful record of the 7 cards and places them upon the sun.
9. C places sun pile on any chosen pile and piles all the cards as directed heretofore. (See page 54.)
10. C cuts 3 times as directed in Sec. 12, 10 seconds apart, *on even time*
11. B quadrates the book as directed in Sec's 13 and 14.
12. B gathers the emblems and C cuts twice, 5 sec. apart.
13. B spreads the grand lay out. See Sec. 16.
14. B finds the ruling grand spread in order to determine the general effect of the time.
15. Turn the 7 planetary cards.
16. Delineate as instructed in the following tables of effects.

Page 76 starts the department of card emblems, definitions and quadratic lay-outs which cover one hundred and four pages of this work.

SOLAR VALUE 1.
SPIRIT VALUE, 10.
ASTRAL NUMBER, 44722.

MERCURY.

A wish for warm love. Longing for affection from opposite sex. News from a friend near at hand. A telegram or telephone message.

VENUS.

A love letter. A letter of friendship. Invitation to a party. Proposal of marriage by letter. A wish for love, friendship and affection. A desire for harmony.

MARS.

A wish to be of help to a friend. News of a friend in trouble. Desire to stand well with some person of strong mind and disposition.

JUPITER.

Desire for money for an unselfish use. Wish to help friends pecuniarily. Letter from a friend regarding some pecuniary favor. A telegram regarding money.

SATURN.

Wish to help some friend in sickness. Desire to aid the afflicted. News of the sickness of a friend. Letter announcing the death of a friend.

URANUS.

Wish to obtain employment of a friendly person. Strong wish regarding labor of some kind. Wish for and love of the occult.

NEPTUNE.

Wish to go upon a journey of friendship. Longing to travel with a friend. Love of the unseen things of nature. Longing for message from a distance.

The Mystic Test Book.

GRAND SPREAD, SOLAR.

QUADRATED TO TIME.

FUTURE.   **PAST.**

SOLAR VALUE, 2.
SPIRIT VALUE, 20.
ASTRAL NUMBER, 36623.

MERCURY.

A sudden passion for one of the opposite sex. Meeting an
old friend unexpectedly. A friendly offer or proposal.
Invitation to a party.

VENUS.

Meeting of dear friends or lovers. Q h, 2 h, J h indicate an
engagement of marriage. 8 h a wedding. A *union
of hearts.*

MARS.

Meeting of lovers, followed by a coolness or quarrel. Soon
ended, however, and all is serene. Followed by a Jack,
indicating a visit from a male friend.

JUPITER.

Two old friends meet. A happy visit soon ended. 2 h, Q h
visit from a lady. If a King or Knave a visit from
a gentleman.

SATURN.

Visit to a sick friend. If 7 s, 9 s, 2 h a meeting at a funeral.
2 h, 8 c influence *from an unseen friend.* Followed by
an ace, a letter from a friend who is ill.

URANUS.

Co-partnership in labor. Union in labor. Work with a
friend. Engagement to labor. A bargain between two
persons. With ace of hearts, a letter regarding work.

NEPTUNE.

Meeting of friends after a long journey. Letter from a
distance. 2 h, 1 h a love letter. Between J-J young
men or sailors meet.

The Mystic  Test Book.

GRAND SPREAD,   QUADRATED TO

ŠOLAR.   TIME.

—o—   —o—

FUTURE.   **PAST.**

SOLAR VALUE,   3.

SPIRIT VALUE,   30.

ASTRAL NUMBER, 15645.

MERCURY.

Indecision of mind regarding love or matrimony. Two lovers at one time. Perplexity regarding your friends. Indecision regarding a visit.

VENUS.

Two lovers at once. Indecision regarding love. Indecision as to attending a place of amusement or instruction. Perplexity of the heart.

MARS.

A proposal of marriage perplexes. Trouble to make up your mind. Two friends quarrel regarding something connected with yourself.

JUPITER.

Perplexity regarding a money matter connected with one you esteem or love. Two ways open at once. Help to a friend, regretted afterwards.

SATURN.

Trouble and concern, worry and indecision, caused by illness of self or friends. Wish to leave home but can not do so.

URANUS.

Trouble and perplexity with work. Two jobs pressing at once. Two roads open to you and you know not which to take.

NEPTUNE.

Indecision relative to a journey. Wish to be in two places at once. Perplexing trouble at a distance. Followed by a Jack, a man you trust causes it.

The Mystic Test Book.

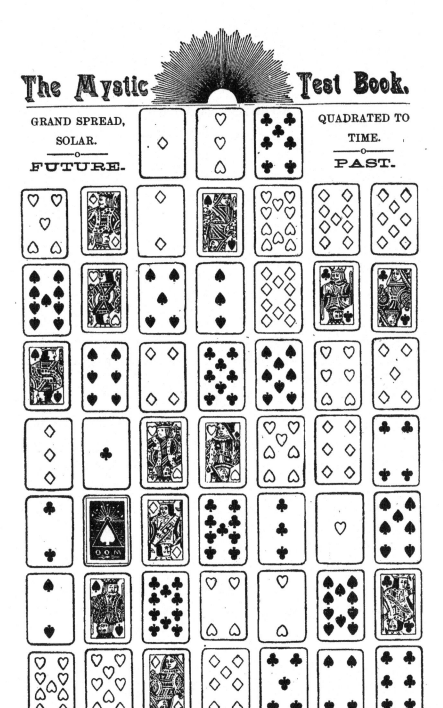

GRAND SPREAD,
SOLAR.

FUTURE.

QUADRATED TO
TIME.

PAST.

SOLAR VALUE,   4.
SPIRIT VALUE,   40.
ASTRAL NUMBER, 54526.

MERCURY.

Satisfaction and success in love. Pleasure in making
new friends. Sudden and unexpected happiness. Pleasure and happiness at home.

VENUS.

Contentment with friendship and love. Satisfaction in love
and a happy home. 4 h, 8 c, 10 h satisfaction and
success in *unseen friends and influences.*

MARS.

Satisfaction in friendly conversation with person of same
sex. Satisfaction gained through law, if law-suit is
shown elsewhere.

JUPITER.

Satisfaction in costly furniture. In fine dresses and a fine
home. Love of fine surroundings. 10 h, 4 h a love for
your new work. 4 h, 10 d pleasure in money making.

SATURN.

Recovery from illness by self or friends. Satisfaction with
visits of unseen friends. Pleasure derived from kind
ness to the sick.

URANUS.

Satisfaction in your employment. Kindness of a friend regarding labor of some kind. Happiness in working for
others.

NEPTUNE.

Satisfaction in travel by water and land. Good luck in
fishing or anything connected with the water. A visit
of pleasant friends from afar.

The Mystic Test Book.

GRAND SPREAD,
SOLAR.

FUTURE.

QUADRATED TO
TIME.

PAST.

SOLAR VALUE,　　5.

SPIRIT VALUE,　　50.

ASTRAL NUMBER,　32333.

MERCURY.

Sudden change in life. Change in feelings. Removal of home somewhat unexpected. Short journey to home of friends.

VENUS.

Change in love or friendship. Parting from friends. Journey to another city or town, K h, 5 h, Q h divorce or separation.

MARS.

Parting from male friends. A journey with a male. Removal for reasons connected with some man. Change of feelings towards a man.

JUPITER.

A business journey. Change in circumstances of a friend or a near relative. 5 h, 1 c, 2 c news of a change comes by letter.

SATURN.

Change of surroundings caused by sickness of friends. 7 s, 9 s, 5 h death is the cause of the change. Journey caused by ill health.

URANUS.

Journey by land. Change of residence. Removal of home and business. Visit of friends from a distance. With an ace, a letter.

NEPTUNE.

Journey by water. Change of home or removal to a place near a body of water. A change connected with transportation and travel.

The Mystic Test Book.

GRAND SPREAD,				QUADRATED TO
SOLAR.				TIME.
—o—				—o—
FUTURE.				PAST.

SOLAR VALUE,   6.
SPIRIT VALUE,   60.
ASTRAL NUMBER, 43593.

MERCURY.

Even temper and dispassionate qualities. Smooth running
life. But few changes. Contra-indicates the five of
hearts under same planet.

VENUS.

Love and friendship running smoothly and without much
variety. Married happiness. Contentment for a
season.

MARS.

Monotony of life and male forces or strength. In some
cases this emblem indicates a long engagement of
marriage.

JUPITER.

Monotony or long continuation of existing pecuniary affairs.
If a co-partnership is shown, it will be long continued.
Slow moving life.

SATURN.

Sickness of friends or relatives or any other condition under
Saturn remains the same. Change, if any, slight under
this ruling.

URANUS.

Matters appertaining to real estate. One's labor, home and
friends remain in a monotonous condition for some
time.

NEPTUNE.

Contra-indicates journeys under same planet or co-ordinating therewith. If business of person is traveling
the indication is reversed.

GRAND SPREAD,
SOLAR.
—o—
FUTURE.

QUADRATED TO
TIME.
—o—
PAST.

SOLAR VALUE 7.
SPIRIT VALUE, 70.
ASTRAL NUMBER, 13138.

MERCURY.

A sudden and generally an unexpected trouble, soon past. Sudden cooling of a friendship. A fever of short duration.

VENUS.

An unfaithful friend or lover. A heart ache caused by a friend. A trouble easily overcome. Illness of some friend.

MARS.

A broken marriage engagement in some cases. A trouble that lasts some weeks. A friend in trouble or a lawsuit.

JUPITER.

Loss through a friend. A friend in some pecuniary trouble. Anxiety caused by money trouble. Illness caused by anxiety.

SATURN.

Illness caused by overwork. Illness of some dear friend. A deep and lasting trouble, A secret. Concealment of a bodily infirmity.

URANUS.

A warning to be cautious. Trouble with labor. Use care in dealings with a friend. A psychic experience. If with a Queen, it is with a lady.

NEPTUNE.

Trouble connected with a journey. Parting from a friend. Inability of self or new friend to make a certain journey.

The Mystic  Test Book.

SOLAR VALUE, 8.
SPIRIT VALUE 80.
ASTRAL NUMBER, 63147.

MERCURY.

Sudden power, soon expended. Opera and dancing parties. Gathering of friends and societies. Power and development of love.

VENUS.

Social and religious gatherings. Spiritual force, power and development. Advancement in soul force. Increase in friendship and love.

MARS.

Gatherings or meetings where males predominate. Strong power. Will force. Martial music. Parties where music is by brass bands.

JUPITER.

Meetings of friends or fraternal societies. Financial power. Consideration of financial questions. Strength or power of expression.

SATURN.

Circles and meetings for psychic investigation. Physicians meetings or societies of like nature. Power in overcoming disease.

URANUS.

Labor of love. Friends working together. Spiritual development and power. Psychic force in conjunction with friends.

NEPTUNE.

Boating parties. Excursions by water. Power in line of something connected with travel. With 1 h and 2 h, good news from afar.

The Mystic Test Book.

GRAND SPREAD,
SOLAR.

—o—

FUTURE.

QUADRATED TO
TIME.

—o—

PAST.

SOLAR VALUE,   9.

SPIRIT VALUE,   1.

ASTRAL NUMBER, 11471.

MERCURY.

A sudden disappointment soon over and gone. Overturning of plans by the action of a trusted friend or employee. A love disappointment.

VENUS.

Disappointment in love. Disappointment in some friend. A heart longing unsatisfied. A misunderstanding. Disaprobation with the conduct of a friend.

MARS.

A lovers' misunderstanding. Disappointment caused by a male friend. Jealousy of another person. Injury to a friend or relative.

JUPITER.

Loss of time in pursuit of love. Disappointment of strong hopes connected with pecuniary affairs of self or near friends.

SATURN.

Misfortune, trouble and disappointment caused by either imprudence, jealousy, lovers' quarrel or illness of self or friends.

URANUS.

Want of success in your labors. Disappointment connected with your work. A labor of love. A friend or relative disappoints you in some work.

NEPTUNE.

A fruitless journey. Disappointment regarding a visit to friends, or in some cases regarding a journey. A disappointing visit from a distance.

The Mystic Test Book.

GRAND SPREAD, SOLAR.				QUADRATED TO TIME.		

FUTURE.    **PAST.**

SOLAR VALUE,   10.
SPIRIT VALUE,   11.
ASTRAL NUMBER, 65418.

MERCURY.

A sudden success. Success in love and friendship. Rapid gaining of friends. Strong affection. If with a Queen, success of a lady friend.

VENUS.

Success, triumph and happiness in friendship and love. A successful love affair. True love from one of the opposite sex for yourself.

MARS.

Reunion of old friends. Success in a friendly negotiation. In some cases triumphs of a friend, in some a law case.

JUPITER.

Power, success, triumph and happiness. Strength of love and friendship. Help and confidence of friends. Business success based on friendly influences.

SATURN,

Power over sickness, sorrow, death, trouble, disappointment, machinations of enemies, scandals and heartburnings. Overcoming or evil influences.

URANUS.

Power, success, and good results flowing from your efforts connected with labor and business affairs. Overcoming of some bad influence, by psychic power.

NEPTUNE.

Success in a journey. Success in fishing, boating or anything connected with the water. Recovery from any illness caused by dampness.

The Mystic Test Book.

GRAND SPREAD,   QUADRATED TO

SOLAR.   TIME.

—o—   —o—

FUTURE.   **PAST.**

SOLAR VALUE,   11.
SPIRIT VALUE,   21.
ASTRAL NUMBER, 27268.

MERCURY.

A lover or very close friend. An affectionate and impulsive young man. A friend in sudden need. In some cases it may indicate a son or brother.

VENUS.

A warm friend or lover. A kind-hearted young man. An amiable gentleman and a true friend. Sometimes a young relative.

MARS.

An amiable and good-hearted young man. Engaged to be married in some cases. Deeply religious or spiritual nature. Strong feelings.

JUPITER.

A kind friend, a man who is of assistance to you in a pecuniary way. A man of strong affection and soul powers.

SATURN.

A good conscientious and true-hearted man, but in trouble and overcome by bad influences. In some cases ill health is the cause.

URANUS.

A kind-hearted and industrious young man. Friendly and helpful. He is usually strong in psychic powers. Sometimes a young lover.

NEPTUNE.

A gentleman of experience, who has traveled and seen much of the world. A lover who has traveled much. Sailors and traveling men are represented by this card.

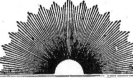

The Mystic Test Book.

GRAND SPREAD,
SOLAR.
—o—
FUTURE.

QUADRATED TO
TIME.
—o—
PAST.

SOLAR VALUE,   12.
SPIRIT VALUE,   31.
ASTRAL NUMBER, 44516.

MERCURY.

A flighty, merry, light-hearted maiden, who loves parties picnics, balls, etc. Sometimes indicates a female flirt. In other cases a sweetheart.

VENUS.

A warm-hearted, loving, faithful woman. Disposition of kindness and self-sacrifice. An affectionate sweetheart.

MARS.

A faithful, warm-hearted wife or mother. Lady who has some male characteristics regarding business matters. Sometimes a strong and healthy young girl.

JUPITER.

A warm-hearted lady of some pecuniary ability and power. A good friend. If matched or co-ordinated with a King, she is married.

SATURN.

An affectionate and warm-hearted widow lady. In some eases a divorced woman, but not through her own fault. Usually, unless contra-indicated, in poor health.

URANUS.

An industrious, good and faithful woman. May be wife, sister or friend only. A loving mother. Gentle disposition and strong psychic powers sometimes.

NEPTUNE.

A good-natured and kindly disposed lady who has traveled a great deal. A good talker. Loves humanity in general. Sometimes rather visionary.

The Mystic Test Book.

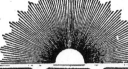

GRAND SPREAD, SOLAR.				QUADRATED TO TIME.
FUTURE.				PAST.

SOLAR VALUE,   13.
SPIRIT VALUE   41.
ASTRAL NUMBER, 44518.

MERCURY.

A middle-aged or elderly gentleman. Quick witted but good tempered and kindly dispositioned. A friend to you.

VENUS.

A mild mannered, kindly, warm-hearted man. A good friend, or in some cases a near relative by blood or marriage. A kind and affectionate husband.

MARS.

A good-hearted man. Usually a married man. A great talker and reasoner. Sometimes a little quick in temper, but soon over it. An old military man in some cases.

JUPITER.

A professional man or merchant of much power and force of character. A friend to you. A man of much power in gaining friends.

SATURN.

A good, kindly dispositioned friend, who is usually a physician, or in some manner associated with sickness and death. Strong psychic powers under Saturn.

URANUS.

A good-hearted, hard working man, who has always worked for the benefit of others. He has powerful psychic forces about him and with him.

NEPTUNE.

A kind-hearted man who has traveled a great deal. A great story teller. Sometimes this card indicates an old sailor.

The Mystic Test Book.

GRAND SPREAD,
SOLAR,
—o—
FUTURE.

QUADRATED TO
TIME.
—o—
PAST.

SOLAR VALUE, 14.
SPIRIT VALUE, 51.
ASTRAL NUMBER, 44731.

MERCURY.

A wish suddenly formed. An aspiration for knowledge. A letter containing a secret. A piece of news from a short distance.

VENUS.

Letter, when in conjunction with deuces. A love of knowledge. A wish gratified. Good news in a letter. A telegram with good news.

MARS.

Desire for much knowledge. Inquisitiveness. Desire for occult communication. Love of power. Letter from a gentleman, when with a deuce.

JUPITER.

Desire for knowledge that may lead to power or preferment. Money or property possessions. With 2 or 5, indicates a business proposition.

SATURN.

Letter containing bad news, especially with 2s and 7s. A wish which will not be gratified. A longing for the unattainable. Bad news from a sick person.

URANUS.

A wish for knowledge regarding some kind of work. Aspirations for advancement in work. Hunger for occult manifestations.

NEPTUNE.

A wish to gain knowledge and experience through travel. If followed by a 2 it indicates a letter from a distance. With J h, news from a traveler far away.

The Mystic Test Book.

GRAND SPREAD,
SOLAR.
———o———
FUTURE.

QUADRATED TO
TIME.
———o———
PAST.

SOLAR VALUE,   15.
SPIRIT VALUE,   61.
ASTRAL NUMBER, 36632.

MERCURY.

Dispute with a hot-headed person. Sudden meeting with a person whom you have had dealings with. With the ace, it means a letter or telegram.

VENUS.

Unions of acquaintances. Joining in study, of two persons' Information regarding a subject of study. Introduction to an intelligent lady.

MARS.

Interview with a gentleman of business. Interview with a reporter. A dispute between two males. A quarrel or lawsuit, under some aspects.

JUPITER.

Interview with a gentleman on pecuniary or business affair. A business proposition. Introduction to business man. Joinings and co-partnerships.

SATURN.

Interview with a physician or lawyer. Conversation with a person who is ill. A quarrel, under some aspects. A bargain with a professional man.

URANUS.

Labor with a person not related to you. Dispute regarding a job of work. Co-partnership in labor. A proposition to use your knowledge for another's benefit.

NEPTUNE.

Introduction to a traveled person. Study with a person from another place. A letter, when with an ace. With a personal card, news from person represented.

The Mystic Test Book.

SOLAR VALUE,　　16.
SPIRIT VALUE,　　`71.
ASTRAL NUMBER, 16545.

MERCURY.

Indecision relative to a short journey. Needed in two places at the same time. Undecided as to two lines of study. Two ways open to you.

VENUS.

Indecision or doubt in an affair of friendship with a lady. Undecided news or doubt regarding a lady friend. Two ways open at once.

MARS.

Indecision regarding a transaction with a gentleman. Doubtful news. Knowledge of an undecided character. If followed by an ace, the news comes by letter.

JUPITER.

Knowledge regarding a financial transaction, is held in doubt. Undecided in mind relative to a certain bargain or proposition.

SATURN.

Indecision, doubt and distrust as to the future, caused by bad influences or ill health. Knowledge of. a doubtful character from two places.

URANUS.

Doubt and a state of unrest and indecision regarding some line of work or appertaining to a real estate transaction. Doubtful psychic experiences.

NEPTUNE.

Indecision relating to a journey to some distance. Doubtful news from far away. Uneasy feeling regarding a distant transaction.

The Mystic Test Book.

GRAND SPREAD, SOLAR.				QUADRATED TO TIME.		
FUTURE.				**PAST.**		

SOLAR VALUE,   17.
SPIRIT VALUE   81.
ASTRAL NUMBER, 54211.

MERCURY.

Happiness lasting but a short time. A pleasant companion
or an interesting book in your company or possession
for a short time only.

VENUS.

Happy home life, comfort and joy. Knowledge of a com-
forting nature. Enjoyment of spiritual or mental
privileges.

MARS.

Pleasant and improving conversations with others, especially
gentlemen. Happy married life or pleasant home surroundings. Good news from home.

JUPITER.

Business contentment. Satisfactory state of money matters.
Satisfactory knowledge of pecuniary affairs. Good
transaction of a financial character.

SATURN.

Good news received from a person who is ill. A happy and
contented person, although in ill health, is indicated.
Goodness and virtue.

URANUS.

Contentment with labor performed. Satisfaction regarding
work done by others. Home life and enjoyment. With
10 d, a satisfactory real estate deal.

NEPTUNE.

A pleasant journey. Good news or knowledge appertaining
to something at a distance. Instructive conversation
with a traveler.

The Mystic   Test Book.

GRAND SPREAD,   QUADRATED TO

SOLAR.   TIME.

——o——   ——o——

FUTURE.   **PAST.**

SOLAR VALUE,   18.
SPIRIT VALUE,   2.
ASTRAL NUMBER, 32342.

MERCURY.

A sudden and unexpected change of feelings. A change in knowledge and mentality. Sudden news received. Journey to place near by.

VENUS.

Sudden change in friendship, which may be either way. Change of mind regarding a certain lady friend. The company of an entertaining friend.

MARS.

A misunderstanding, causing a change in one's life. Change of opinion regarding a gentleman. A slight quarrel. With 2 c, news of a change in affairs.

JUPITER.

A change in pecuniary affairs. Change in the circumstances of a debtor causes a change in your calculations. With a *ten*, the change will be for the better.

SATURN.

Change of plans caused by ill health of self or others. Journey, or short trip, for health, or to see a sick friend. Discontent.

URANUS.

A journey, by land only. Change in one's home life. Sale of real estate. Change in mental or psychic powers. Change in knowledge, regarding real estate.

NEPTUNE.

A long journey over land and water. A trip by water. News or knowledge of events that are transpiring at a distance.

The Mystic Test Book.

GRAND SPREAD,
SOLAR.
——o——
FUTURE.

QUADRATED TO
TIME.
——o——
PAST.

SOLAR VALUE,　　19.
SPIRIT VALUE,　　12.
ASTRAL NUMBER, 44736.

MERCURY.

Unchangeableness or monotony, lasting for a few days only. Steadfast confidence and esteem for friends. Remaining quiet at home.

VENUS.

Uniform and unchanging friendship. Knowledge and surroundings remain the same as heretofore. Lack of news. Quiet monotony of life.

MARS.

Absence of trouble, quarrels and changes, affecting males principally. Study and improvement goes on steadily and uniformly.

JUPITER.

Monotony in business matters. Pecuniary affairs at a standstill, no matter whether good or bad. A lack of news regarding a business transaction.

SATURN,

Uniform health or the contrary, according to preceding conditions. Lack of change in the sick. With physicians this card indicates uniformity in business.

URANUS.

Unchangeableness in home life, physical and mental surroundings. Monotony in study and labor. This card neutralizes the 5 of clubs.

NEPTUNE.

Lack of change relative to travel. Contra-indicates journeys under same or co-ordinate planets. Neutralizes a five under Mercury in same life line.

The Mystic Test Book.

GRAND SPREAD, SOLAR.				QUADRATED TO TIME.

FUTURE.   **PAST.**

SOLAR VALUE,　　20.

SPIRIT VALUE,　　22.

ASTRAL NUMBER, 15253.

MERCURY.

A trouble that comes suddenly. Bad news from a distance. Inharmony of feelings. Opposition to your projects. An obstacle to gaining knowledge.

VENUS.

Unfulfilled hopes. Some kind of trouble or quarrel with a woman. Opposition to some belief held by you. A rejected favor or request.

MARS.

Opposition from a male. A quarrel or a lawsuit. Trouble in gaining certain knowledge. Antagonism to your wishes and projects.

JUPITER.

Trouble on account of some business transaction. Bad news regarding a mercantile firm or corporation Antagonism from some business firm.

SATURN.

A scandal. Backbiting. Ill remarks regarding the person. Illness caused by worry or overstudy. Overthrowing of your plans for advancement in knowledge.

URANUS.

Misinformation regarding a piece of work. Trouble with a job of work. Trouble regarding real estate. Antagonizing influences of a psychic nature.

NEPTUNE.

Bad news from far away. Trouble with some matter at a distance. An important letter. Antagonizing influences, that come from some one far away.

The Mystic Test Book.

GRAND SPREAD, SOLAR.				QUADRATED TO TIME.

—o—

FUTURE.

PAST.

SOLAR VALUE,   21.
SPIRIT VALUE,   32.
ASTRAL NUMBER, 63642.

MERCURY.

Rapid gaining of knowledge. A rapid development. Meetings for purposes of advancement. Strength and courage. Overcoming of obstacles to advancement.

VENUS.

Feminine advancement in favor of gaining knowledge.
Spiritual development or psychic powers. Represents
female schools or gatherings.

MARS.

Debates. Male strength and power. Psychic unfoldment
and advancement. Represents male schools or gatherings sometimes, of men, for political or other purposes.

JUPITER.

Councils and meetings for financial consideration of questions. Power and knowledge, applied to some money
making scheme or business

SATURN.

Power to overcome illness or trouble, through knowledge
and development. Recovery of a friend who has been ill.
Good news from a sick acquaintance.

URANUS.

Meetings and gatherings of persons for the consideration
of questions connected with labor. Power and knowledge of business or labor. News regarding real estate.

NEPTUNE.

Knowledge of matters connected with travel or water.
Ability to succeed in such avocations as come under
that head.

The Mystic Test Book.

GRAND SPREAD, SOLAR.				QUADRATED TO TIME.

FUTURE.   **PAST.**

SOLAR VALUE,   22.
SPIRIT VALUE,   42.
ASTRAL NUMBER, 24926.

MERCURY.

A sudden disappointment and bad news. Knowledge of a dissatisfying nature. A sudden dislike. Discouragement caused by antagonism to you.

VENUS.

Disappointment regarding a personal friend; usually a female, under this planet. Disappointment in gaining knowledge. Friendly antagonism to your projects.

MARS.

Dislike, distaste, disbelief of some person or thing you are brought into contact with. In some cases a lawsuit. Disappointment caused by lack of knowledge.

JUPITER.

Discontent with one's pecuniary affairs. News of money matters, that is disappointing to you. With 7 d, loss of property by the disappointment.

SATURN.

Disappointment, discontent or some disquieting feeling caused by illness of self or some one connected with you. Disappointment in gaining knowledge; caused by illness.

URANUS.

Disappointment connected with one's business or labor. In some cases a wish to change avocation. Psychic experience of a disappointing character.

NEPTUNE.

Disappointment regarding a journey. Generally a long journey, all or partly by water. Discontent with residence. This card neutralizes the 10, of same suit.

The Mystic Test Book.

| GRAND SPREAD, SOLAR. —o— FUTURE. | | | | QUADRATED TO TIME. —o— PAST. |

SOLAR VALUE, 23.
SPIRIT VALUE, 52.
ASTRAL NUMBER, 65751.

MERCURY.

A sudden and sometimes unexpected success. Good news. Success in gaining knowledge. This card neutralizes a 7 c or 9 c next to it.

VENUS.

Success in friendship. Success in uniting with others in gaining some kind of knowledge or mental growth. Indicates or predicts good news.

MARS.

Success in married life. Also in study at home. Applies more particularly to males, however. General success in professional avocations.

JUPITER.

Success and contentment in merchantile or business avocations. Advanced knowledge in your business. Success through learning and mind force.

SATURN.

Strength, power and success against the evil effects of Saturn. Overcomes bad influences through knowledge of men and things.

URANUS

Contentment in success, connected with labor. Success in a real estate transaction. General success in agriculture and kindred pursuits.

NEPTUNE.

Success on the water. Successful knowledge relating to travel or some affair at a distance. Indicates knowledge necessary for success in traveling.

The Mystic  Test Book.

GRAND SPREAD, SOLAR.				QUADRATED TO TIME.

FUTURE.   **PAST.**

SOLAR VALUE,   24.
SPIRIT VALUE,   62.
ASTRAL NUMBER, 27844.

MERCURY.

A quick-witted and intelligent young man. In some cases a
rival to the person. In some cases a lawyer friend.
With odd diamonds at each side, a business rival.

VENUS.

A jealous young man. Represents one who is full of life.
A sharp, bold eyed man. With females, this card indicates a suitor.

MARS.

A quarrelsome man. A plotter against some person or
persons nearly connected with you. Sometimes an
attorney at law.

JUPITER.

A man who is making money through his peculiar knowl
edge regarding a certain line of business. Sometimes
indicates a business rival.

SATURN.

A rather dissolute young man. Keeps late hours. In some
cases it indicates a man you should beware of. With
7 c and 8 c, a studious young man who is in poor health.

URANUS.

An industrious young man who has a good knowledge of his
business. In some cases a real estate dealer. In certain
aspects it represents an intelligent farmer.

NEPTUNE.

A jolly rover. A traveling man. In some cases a sailor,
lively and full of fun. A young man who possesses
knowledge of a wide range.

The Mystic Test Book.

GRAND SPREAD,
SOLAR.

FUTURE.

QUADRATED TO
TIME.

PAST.

SOLAR VALUE,   25.

SPIRIT VALUE,   72.

ASTRAL NUMBER, 43472.

MERCURY.

A smart, lively lady, intelligent and quick witted. Loves parties and plays. A rapid reader. Represents a lady, possessing knowledge of an unusual character.

VENUS.

An intelligent, accomplished lady, of strong religious or psychic proclivities. Sometimes a beautiful singer or musician.

MARS.

A smart woman, but rather quick tempered. In some cases she presents a rather masculine disposition or appearance. A lady of strong will force and power.

JUPITER.

A lady of strong powers and force of character. Generally one who makes her own way in the world. A business woman.

SATURN.

An intelligent lady, but one who has experienced much sickness and trouble. Sometimes indicates a jealous woman.

URANUS

A hard working, industrious lady, who brings knowledge to bear in her work. One who earns money for herself. In some cases, a farmer's wife.

NEPTUNE.

A traveled lady. One who has seen much of the world and has profited thereby. A lady who possesses knowledge that fits her for a stirring life.

The Mystic Test Book.

<table>
<tr>
<td>GRAND SPREAD,
SOLAR.
—o—
FUTURE.</td>
<td></td>
<td></td>
<td></td>
<td>QUADRATED TO
TIME.
—o—
PAST.</td>
</tr>
</table>

SOLAR VALUE, 26.
SPIRIT VALUE, 82.
ASTRAL NUMBER, 43474.

MERCURY.

A quick tempered man. Smart, lively and witty man. Quick to grasp a point. *Kings generally represent married men or men of middle or advanced age.*

VENUS.

A kind-hearted and even tempered gentleman. Usually one who is learned, or following some learned profession. Represents a man of middle age.

MARS.

A loud talking overbearing man. Sometimes a military man, or one who leads or commands. A smart, active office holder or politician.

JUPITER.

An intelligent reasoner and powerful speaker. In some cases a physician or lawyer. Shows generally a man of "power." With diamonds strong, a merchant.

SATURN.

Usually a physician, but one who is not sympathetic. Rather hard-hearted. Inclined to be cross and exacting. An old gentleman who has been a learned man.

URANUS.

One who has studied hard and read a great deal. One who has much will power and psychic force. An intelligent worker.

NEPTUNE.

An old sailor or sea captain. A smart traveling man. A lover of out door sports, boating, fishing, etc. In some cases a learned man from a distant place.

The Mystic  Test Book.

GRAND SPREAD,
SOLAR.
——o——
FUTURE.

QUADRATED TO
TIME.
——o——
PAST.

SOLAR VALUE,   27.
SPIRIT VALUE,   3.
ASTRAL NUMBER, 23113.

MERCURY.

A wish to make money rapidly. A telegram or letter regarding pecuniary matters. A sudden aspiration connected with money.

VENUS.

Desire for money to be used for a kindly purpose. Wish to
do good with wealth. Unselfish wish for wealth. With
a *ten*, the wish will be gratified.

MARS.

Wish for money connected in some way with the law. Aspiration to succeed in some branch of law. Money letter
from a man

JUPITER.

Important message on business. Wish, connected with a
large business transaction. Strong aspiration for
success in business.

SATURN.

Wish to succeed, which is destined to be disappointed, unless
strong indications point the other way. Letter or telegram regarding illness of some person.

URANUS.

Wish for chance to earn money by labor. Aspiration to
succeed in some work to be undertaken. Letter regarding labor matters, when followed by a 2 s or 2 d.

NEPTUNE.

Message from a distance. Wish for success connected with
travel or business at a distance. News from far away.
A wish for money to be used in making a journey.

The Mystic Test Book.

GRAND SPREAD,
SOLAR.
——o——
FUTURE.

QUADRATED TO
TIME.
——o——
PAST.

SOLAR VALUE,   28.
SPIRIT VALUE,   13.
ASTRAL NUMBER, 32348.

MERCURY.

A business arrangement very suddenlv concluded: An unexpected pecuniary offer. A business interview. A. telegram on business.

VENUS.

Introduction to a lady of means. Business arrangement wherein at least one party is a female. Co-partnership with a friend.

MARS.

Consultation with a lawyer. Pecuniary bargain with a male. Union of business interests. A business meeting. A letter regarding money.

JUPITER.

Business consultation. A ,pecuniary co-partnership. A combination. Union of monied interests. Business meeting.

SATURN.

Interview with a physician. A demand for money. A dunning letter. A bill. An unlucky pecuniary affair. With *sevens* of any suit, bad news of some kind.

URANUS.

Consultation regarding labor. Profitable union of labor interests. Business and labor combined. Labor co-partnership. A real estate transaction.

NEPTUNE.

Consultation regarding a business journey. Engagement to travel for another. Money from a distance, particularly when followed by a 4 d or 10 d.

The Mystic Test Book.

GRAND SPREAD,   QUADRATED TO

SOLAR.   TIME.

—0—

FUTURE.   **PAST.**

SOLAR VALUE 29.

SPIRIT VALUE 23.

ASTRAL NUMBER, 16311.

MERCURY.

A sudden indecision arrises regarding a pecuniary matter. Two business ways open at once. A feeling of uneasy insecurity. Doubt and distrust regarding business.

VENUS.

Indecision relating to money affairs and a lady. Regarding a certain friend and a money matter. Choice between two propositions.

MARS.

An undecided pecuniary affair with a male. A lawsuit in a state of uncertainty. An uncertain trouble arises. Doubt regarding a pecuniary transaction.

JUPITER.

An undecided business investment. Indecision connected with a large transaction. Two ways open at once in pecuniary affairs. Uncertainty and doubt.

SATURN.

Uncertainty caused by death, or perhaps only illness. A feeling of insecurity regarding future pecuniary transaction.

URANUS.

A real estate transaction held in suspense. Uncertain outcome to a labor matter. Two ways open at once. Choice of two kinds of labor, both fair.

NEPTUNE.

Uncertainty and indecision connected with money, a journey or some matter at a distance. Doubt and general indecision regarding future home and business.

**GRAND SPREAD,
SOLAR.**

——o——

FUTURE.

**QUADRATED TO
TIME.**

——o——

PAST.

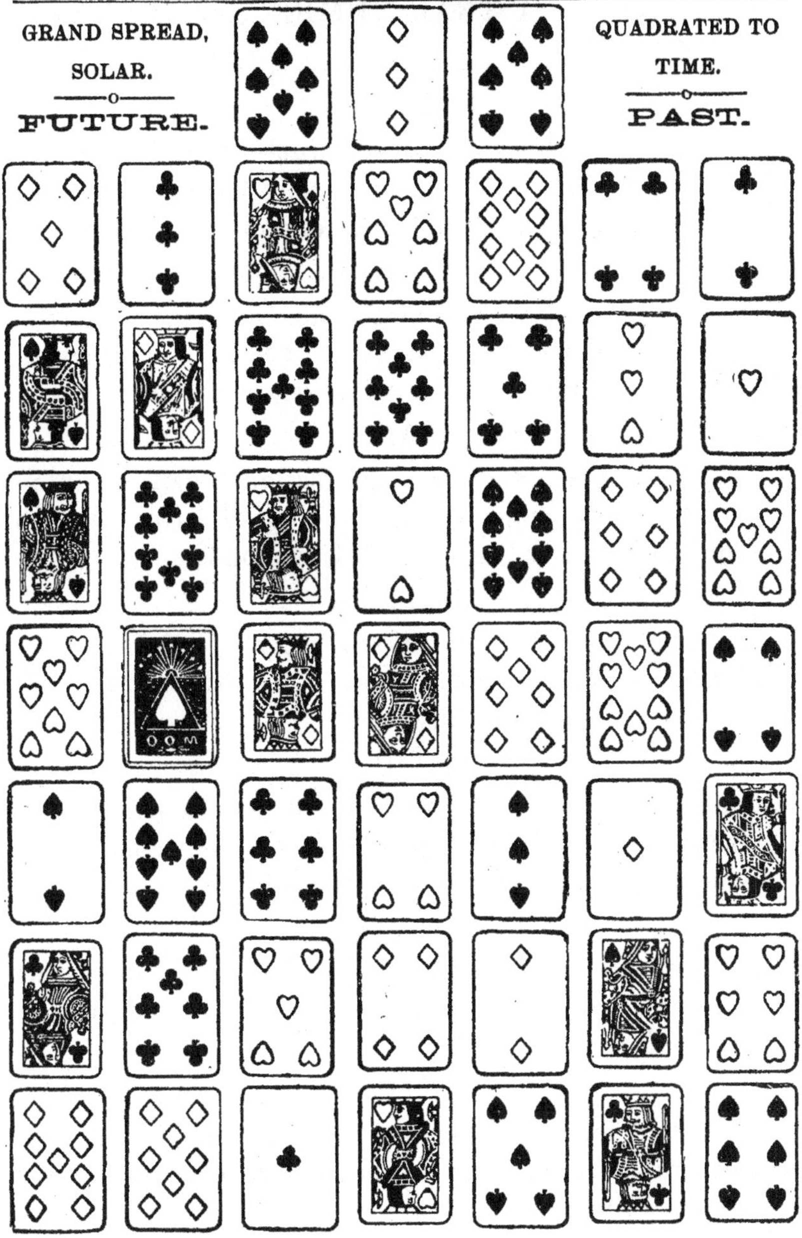

SOLAR VALUE,   30.

SPIRIT VALUE,   33.

ASTRAL NUMBER, 43771.

MERCURY.

Your hopes will be suddenly realized. Satisfaction in a pecuniary affair. Indecision comes to an end. Sudden receipt of money when hardly expected.

VENUS.

Satisfaction regarding a money affair and a lady. In some cases a dear friend. Adjustment of pecuniary difficulties. General satisfaction of mind as regards money.

MARS.

Termination of a law case. Satisfaction regarding money and a certain man. Happy ending of a trouble. This card counteracts the 5 and 7 of diamonds.

JUPITER.

An investment turns out satisfactorily. Satisfaction obtained connected with money. A good business. Expresses general good business.

SATURN.

Lost money restored. A recovery of health causes satisfaction in a pecuniary way. A will in person's favor, when it follows a seven of spades, especially.

URANUS.

Work prospers. Satisfaction in your labor. Pleasant business prospects. Happy work. Money gained by labor. A satisfactory real estate deal.

NEPTUNE.

A satisfactory journey. Matters turn out well at a distance. Satisfaction regarding business connected with travel. Money gained by travel.

The Mystic Test Book.

GRAND SPREAD,
SOLAR.

FUTURE.

QUADRATED TO
TIME.

PAST.

SOLAR VALUE,   31.
SPIRIT VALUE,   43.
ASTRAL NUMBER, 34133.

MERCURY.

A sudden or unexpected change, affecting the pecuniary status or arrangements of person, or one connected in a business way.

VENUS.

Change in love or friendship, caused by some pecuniary considerations. Financial change connected with a lady or dear friend. Followed by 10 d, the change is a good one.

MARS.

Change happening to a male. A journey on business. A money transaction changes in consequence of the interference of a gentleman in same business.

JUPITER.

A business journey. Change of business. Financial change. Change of an investment. A pecuniary cross to bear, in some cases.

SATURN.

Change of business, location or advantage through sickness misfortune or death. This card is counteracted by the 6 d under Saturn.

URANUS.

Change of location of one's labor. A change of home. A long journey by land. A real estate transaction. This card represents a pecuniary change of some sort.

NEPTUNE.

A change of a pecuniary character, appearing sometimes at a distance. A long journey on business. This card is counteracted by 6 d or 6 s under planet Neptune.

The Mystic  Test Book.

<table>
<tr><td>GRAND SPREAD,
SOLAR.
—o—
FUTURE.</td><td></td><td></td><td></td><td>QUADRATED TO
TIME.
—o—
PAST.</td></tr>
</table>

SOLAR VALUE,   32.
SPIRIT VALUE   53.
ASTRAL NUMBER,   44583.

MERCURY.

Matters will soon settle down smoothly in a financial way.
You will not make a business journey at present.
Counteracts the five of diamonds.

VENUS.

Money affairs move strongly in a monotonous way. No particular change with friends. Contra-indicates the five of
hearts and diamonds under Venus.

MARS.

Affects money matters of males principally. Settlement of
financial difficulties. Smooth moving of financial
arrangements. Counteracts the 5 d and 7 d under Mars.

JUPITER.

Settlement of accounts. Business matters running slowly
along. Remain unchanged whether good or bad. Expresses general lack of excitement

SATURN.

Monotonous life which is quite apt to lead to ennui or illness.
Sameness or want of change in pecuniary affairs.
Counteracts the 5 and 7 of diamonds.

URANUS.

Location of work remains the same. Monotonous labor.
Real estate matters in *statu quo*. Counteracts the five
of diamonds and the five of spades.

NEPTUNE.

Chances for travel very poor. Counteracts one five under
this planet. With two fives, it indicates a monotonous
and long journey on business.

The Mystic Test Book.

GRAND SPREAD,
SOLAR.
——o——
FUTURE.

QUADRATED TO
TIME.
——o——
PAST.

SOLAR VALUE, 33.
SPIRIT VALUE, 63.
ASTRAL NUMBER, 13318.

MERCURY.

Unexpected call for money. Trouble regarding a pecuniary matter. Sudden and unexpected loss of money or property of some kind.

VENUS.

Money paid or given to a lady. Trouble connected with money and a friend, or near relative. With 8 h, money paid out for some pleasure.

MARS.

Loss of money through the law. Money paid out to a man. In some cases a lawsuit, when with 7 c, especially. Indicates trouble connected with money, generally.

JUPITER.

Investment of money in some place where you will not see it again soon. Loss of money in a trade. Use care when this card comes under Jupiter.

SATURN.

Loss of money through illness of self or some other person. Misfortune or bad acts of another. If followed by 7 s and 10 s it is by death of some one.

URANUS.

Money paid out for labor. Investment in land. Paid out for some psychic manifestation. Loss of money for labor done.

NEPTUNE.

Money paid out or entirely lost through something connected with travel or some operation at a distance. Counteracts the eight of diamonds.

The Mystic  Test Book.

—o—

FUTURE.

QUADRATED TO TIME.

—o—

PAST.

SOLAR VALUE,   34.

SPIRIT VALUE,   73.

ASTRAL NUMBER, 63651.

MERCURY.

Sudden accession of power. Rapid gaining of ends sought,
when related to money matters. Meetings for pecuniary
purposes. Overcoming of trouble shown by 7 d.

VENUS.

Power of gaining property through the ability to make
friends. Indicates female financial ability. Money
made through psychic gifts.

MARS.

Power gained through numbers. Meetings of males for
financial consideration of questions. Strength, finan-
cially and commercially.

JUPITER.

Meetings of stockholders and companies, corporations and
societies. Power and ability to make money. Sometimes represents quite large pecuniary transactions.

SATURN.

Meetings of physicians. Power and financial ability connected with illness or death. In most cases represents
gain by what is a loss to others.

URANUS.

Labor meetings. Power of making money through labor.
Power gained through psychic gifts. To make money
through power of foresight.

NEPTUNE.

Power to gain money through travel. Sale of goods or
property at a distance. Financial power in large
concerns extending to far-away places

The Mystic  Test Book.

GRAND SPREAD,
SOLAR.

—o—

FUTURE.

QUADRATED TO
TIME

—o—

PAST.

SOLAR VALUE,   35.
SPIRIT VALUE   83.
ASTRAL NUMBER, 14486.

MERCURY.

Financial disappointment, generally coming suddenly or connected with some speculation. Disappointment regarding a short journey.

VENUS.

Disappointment of a lady, connected in some way with money. Love affair goes wrong on account of finances. Counteracted by 8 d or 10 d under Venus.

MARS.

Disappointment of a gentleman in some financial way. Pecuniary dissatisfaction and trouble. Loss of money by a lawsuit in certain aspects.

JUPITER

Loss of money through some mercantile transaction. Investment of money that will bring no return in cash or property.

SATURN.

Investment in some losing enterprise. Disappointment of hopes regarding financial matters, caused by illness and in some aspects by death.

URANUS.

Disappointment connected with a deal in real estate. Loss of money on labor. In some cases loss of a job or position where labor is employed.

NEPTUNE.

Disappointment connected with travel or a long journey, caused by financial trouble. Money paid out for travel, sometimes.

The Mystic Test Book.

GRAND SPREAD, SOLAR.				QUADRATED TO TIME.		
FUTURE.				**PAST.**		

SOLAR VALUE,   36.

SPIRIT VALUE,   4.

ASTRAL NUMBER, 43647.

MERCURY.

Success in a speculation. Financial success coming suddenly. Success of a short journey. A "streak of good
fortune."

VENUS.

In some aspects a wealthy marriage. A wealthy acquaintance. Success in friends and money. Kind help of
a friend in some cases.

MARS.

Success in a lawsuit. Financial success of a male connected
with person. In some cases represents money gained by
matrimony.

JUPITER.

General success in financial matters. Shows the planets
to be favorable for pecuniary enterprises of any or
all kinds, unless the card is aspected against.

SATURN.

Success in money matters, but will not long continue. Success impeded through ill health, or death of some other
person.

URANUS.

General success in a pecuniary way with labor, business
and real property. Success in selling property. Success in occult matters and those connected with land.

NEPTUNE.

Success in gaining money by travel. Selling goods on
the road by sample. Also in business connected with
the water, such as shipping.

The Mystic Test Book.

SOLAR VALUE,　　37.

SPIRIT VALUE,　　· 14.

ASTRAL NUMBER, 25261.

MERCURY.

A young man who spends money freely and makes money easily. In some cases a railroad man, or connected with something rapid.

VENUS.

A gentleman with a good income. A generous man. A' free-hearted lover or young friend. In some cases a clerk in a business house.

MARS.

Usually a young married man. Sometimes a middle aged single man. An attorney at law. A law clerk. A bank clerk or cashier.

JUPITER.

A well-to-do man. A merchant, salesman, banker, cashier, broker or something of that nature. One who handles considerable money.

SATURN.

A man who has fine business qualities, but is hampered by ill health. In some cases this emblem indicates a wild dissipated man.

URANUS.

An industrious young man who makes considerable money, by his own exertions. In some aspects, a writer who makes money by his pen.

NEPTUNE.

A man who makes money by traveling. In general terms a traveling salesman or agent for some monied concern.

The Mystic Test Book.

SOLAR VALUE,   38.
SPIRIT VALUE,   24.
ASTRAL NUMBER, 33842.

MERCURY.

A lady who loves excitement; parties, operas and every place
where wealth is displayed. She loves money and
luxury.

VENUS.

A warm-hearted, charitable lady who has considerable means.
In some cases a wealthy lady friend of person. In some
aspects an actress or singer.

MARS.

Usually a married lady. One who spends money freely.
She is fond of dress and generally quite pleased with the
admiration of the opposite sex.

JUPITER.

A wealthy lady, or one who is closely connected with
a gentleman who handles money. Such as a business
man or banker.

SATURN.

A lady with money or business ability, but hampered by ill
health. In some cases she is a physician. This card is
an excellent one for physicians, under Saturn.

URANUS.

An industrious and energetic lady who makes money by her
own exertions. In some cases she has strong psychic or
occult gifts which she utilizes.

NEPTUNE.

A traveled lady; one who has spent a great deal of money in
seeing the world. In some cases an actress or opera
singer.

The Mystic Test Book.

GRAND SPREAD,
SOLAR.

——o——

FUTURE.

QUADRATED TO
TIME.

——o——

PAST.

SOLAR VALUE,   39.
SPIRIT VALUE,   34.
ASTRAL NUMBER, 37651.

MERCURY.

A sharp, quick, active, money-making business man. Sometimes a speculator. One who makes money fluctuatingly.

VENUS.

A wealthy lover. A wealthy friend. An actor or musician. A business man with kind heart, who makes much money.

MARS.

In some cases a wealthy husband. A well-to-do lawyer, or one who owns or controls mines and minerals. A man of strong money-making power.

JUPITER.

A wealthy, money-making, proud, "self-made" man, who, as has been said, "loves his maker." In some cases a banker, wholesale dealer or manufacturer.

SATURN

A rich man who is very close with his money. In some cases a miserly man. Under some aspects a man of wealth who is in ill health.

URANUS.

A wealthy man who labors hard to make more money. In some cases a large real estate dealer. A gentleman of much psychic power.

NEPTUNE

A man who has spent much money in travel. Sometimes a merchant or seafaring man who has made a great deal of money.

The Mystic Test Book.

GRAND SPREAD,
SOLAR.

FUTURE.

QUADRATED TO
TIME.

PAST.

SOLAR VALUE, 40.
SPIRIT VALUE, 44.
ASTRAL NUMBER, 56575.

MERCURY.

A secret. wish. A secret resolution. A secret knowledge. A secret society. With mystics it represents the *Order of the Magi.*

VENUS.

A letter containing a secret. A secret love. A secret wish. A secret friend. A secret or occult society or secret order. A secret present to person.

MARS.

A secret shared by a male. A marriage secret. A secret wish. A secret communication. A letter with bad news in some cases. A conspiracy or plot.

JUPITER.

A secret mercantile business or speculative transaction. A secret personal business letter. An important letter. A secret order.

SATURN.

Bad news by letter. A secret communication. In some cases a secret disease or a concealed trouble. A concealed disappointment. A secret kept from you.

URANUS.

A secret journey by land. A secret real estate transaction. Secret or occult psychic power. A secret present. A hidden will.

NEPTUNE.

A journey by water on secret business. News of a private nature from a distance. A letter on private business. Visit of a person on some secret mission.

The Mystic Test Book.

**GRAND SPREAD,
SOLAR.**

—o—

FUTURE.

**QUADRATED TO
TIME.**

—o—

PAST.

SOLAR VALUE, 41.
SPIRIT VALUE, 54.
ASTRAL NUMBER, 36731.

MERCURY.

A pressing engagement. An agreement to work for another. An unexpected offer of a piece of work. A sudden union.

VENUS.

A union with a lady in some kind of work. A joining of forces. A proposal of a business nature. A co-partnership with a relative or near friend.

MARS.

Work in conjunction with a man. Consultation with a lawyer. A combination or plot. A letter from a male. A union of male forces in some kind of labor.

JUPITER.

Interview with a business man relating to work. Letter regarding a piece of work. A transaction between two persons,

SATURN.

Letter announcing the illness of a person you are interested in. News regarding a sick friend. Consultation with a physician. A business call on the sick.

URANUS.

Work done by two persons jointly. Letter regarding a piece of work. News of the illness of a person at a distance, by land. Plan of work between two.

NEPTUNE.

Interview with a person regarding travel on business. News from a distance over water and land. A work at a distance from your residence.

The Mystic  Test Book.

| GRAND SPREAD, SOLAR. —o— FUTURE. | | | | QUADRATED TO TIME. —o— PAST. |

SOLAR VALUE,   42.

SPIRIT VALUE,   64.

ASTRAL NUMBER, 13161.

MERCURY.

A case arrises suddenly where you must decide between two courses. Two ways open at once. Two offers of some kind, relating to work.

VENUS.

Indecision regarding a matter of work or health, connected with a woman. Undecided bargain with a friend. Indecision regarding a home.

MARS.

Undecided business matter. Business indecision. Two ways open in business, both requiring much work. In decision regarding a law case.

JUPITER.

Indecision regarding a cash transaction. Two kinds of business, both requiring much cash to conduct, open up at once for the person.

SATURN.

Indecision caused by a death or illness. An undecided case of illness. An unsettled bill, in some cases. A lingering illness.

URANUS.

Indecision relative to a psychic experience, a real estate transaction, a job of work, a land journey or the conduct of some employee.

NEPTUNE.

Indecision regarding a journey by water, a business at a distance. The visit of a friend, a job of work on the water, or connected with transportation.

The Mystic Test Book.

GRAND SPREAD,
SOLAR.

—o—

FUTURE.

QUADRATED TO
TIME.

—o—

PAST.

SOLAR VALUE, 43.
SPIRIT VALUE, 74.
ASTRAL NUMBER, 54472.

MERCURY.

Realizations of expectations coming suddenly. Unlooked for success in some piece of work. A case decided suddenly. Satisfaction, of limited duration.

VENUS.

Love for your work. Work for others through love for them. Satisfaction in your labors. A happy home life. Contentment of soul.

MARS.

Married happiness for females. Strength in labor of love for males. Satisfactory labor at home. Counteracts the five of spades and seven of spades.

JUPITER.

Satisfactory labor. Good pecuniary returns therefor. Reasonable compensation for labor performed and satisfaction gained thereby.

SATURN.

Recovery from illness. Satisfactory ending of a trouble or disappointment. Counteracts the seven of spades under same planet.

URANUS.

Satisfaction derived from one's business or labor. Satisfaction from news received from a distance. Labor connected with the farm.

NEPTUNE.

Success in travel connected with business or labor. Satisfactory journey by water, when a five comes under the same or a co-ordinate planet.

The Mystic Test Book.

GRAND SPREAD, SOLAR.				QUADRATED TO TIME.
FUTURE.				PAST.

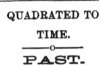

SOLAR VALUE,		44.

SPIRIT VALUE,		84.

ASTRAL NUMBER, 27824.

MERCURY.

A sudden journey. A change of employment. A change in business methods. News regarding a distant transaction.

VENUS.

Change in the labor of a female. Journey of a lady by land. Removal of home or habitation. Visit of a female. A short journey.

MARS.

Change in employment of a male. Visit of a male from a city. A journey connected with business or one's labor. A change in one's usual life and home surroundings.

JUPITER.

Change in pecuniary affairs. Pecuniary change in one's labor. Journey on business. News of a business nature.

SATURN.

Change of employment caused by illness of self or friends. A journey or removal caused by an illness. In some cases it represents an unfortunate journey.

URANUS

Journey connected with business, profession or labor. Change in one's profession or work. A change, ronnected with real estate or agriculture.

NEPTUNE.

Journey to a distance, professional or connected with some kind of work. News from a distance regarding a change.

The Mystic Test Book.

GRAND SPREAD,
SOLAR.
—o—
FUTURE.

QUADRATED TO
TIME.
—o—
PAST.

SOLAR VALUE, 45.
SPIRIT VALUE, 5.
ASTRAL NUMBER, 44754.

MERCURY.

Counteracts changes shown under same planet. End to
worry. Settlement of difficulties. Steady and satisfac
tory employment.

VENUS.

Quiet, uneventful life as regards self and intimate friends
and surroundings. Matters move smoothly. This
card indicates quiet and comfort for females.

MARS.

Settlement of lawsuits, quarrels or anything of the kind
shown under this planet. Absence of change or excitement generally

JUPITER.

Monotony in business or professional life. Business moving
smoothly. Counteracts fives and sevens under same
planet.

SATURN.

Recovery from illness when same is shown. Counteracts
changes and troubles shown under this planet. Followed
ed by 4 d, satisfactory and steady employment.'

URANUS.

Prosperity in profession or labor, or the contrary, remains
without change for some time. Monotony in profession
or labor

NEPTUNE.

If a journey is shown it is a long and dreary one. In
general this emblem indicates " no journey will be made."
Contra-indicates the five and seven of same suit.

The Mystic Test Book.

GRAND SPREAD,
SOLAR.
—o—
FUTURE.

QUADRATED TO
TIME.
—o—
PAST.

SOLAR VALUE,　　46.
SPIRIT VALUE,　　15.
ASTRAL NUMBER, 17782.

MERCURY.

Headache, severe throbbing. Trouble in some matter connected with your work. Sudden accident or illness. Counteracts the eight of spades.

VENUS.

Illness caused by overdoing, late hours or excitement. A love, trouble or illness of a dear friend. Counteracts the seven of hearts.

MARS.

Illness caused by excitement, drink, late hours, passion or severe labor. Chills, cold feet and hands. Represents trouble for males and for females trouble caused by males.

JUPITER.

Illness caused by business worry. Indicates considerable trouble and care. Sleeplessness, headache, pain in the loins and back.

SATURN

Illness and trouble connected with the rulings under Scorpio. This class of diseases need not be particularized here. Followed by a 4 d, a will in your favor.

URANUS.

Trouble with one's work or profession. An obstacle to overcome. Illness caused by overwork. Some work is not satisfactory.

NEPTUNE.

Illness similar to sea sickness. Rheumatism and other diseases caused by dampness. Dropsy. Trouble, or some obstacle, to a journey.

The Mystic Test Book.

FUTURE.

QUADRATED TO TIME.

PAST.

SOLAR VALUE,   47.
SPIRIT VALUE,   25.
ASTRAL NUMBER, 63388.

MERCURY.

Power to control and carry on profession or labor. Rapid accomplishment of work. Overcoming of an obstacle. Ability to succeed against antagonistic circumstances.

VENUS.

Power in overcoming obstacles. Female power and strength of will. A labor of love. Female organizations. Meetings of females for purposes of work in some cause.

MARS.

Organizations of males. Power gained through concentration of forces. Development of power. Overcoming of obstacles.

JUPITER.

Power represented by organizations such as manufacturing companies, railroad corporations and labor organizations. Power and strength in numbers.

SATURN.

Power in overcoming illness and obstacles to advancement. Recovery from illness, when such exists at the time of the delineating.

URANUS.

Strength and power in professional or other labor. Ability to overcome all obstacles. Organized labor. Concentration of forces.

NEPTUNE.

Travel that affects numbers of people and business interests at a distance. Concentrated effort at a distance. Control of laborers in large numbers.

The Mystic Test Book.

**GRAND SPREAD,
SOLAR.**

—o—

FUTURE.

**QUADRATED TO
TIME.**

—o—

PAST.

SOLAR VALUE, 48.
SPIRIT VALUE, 35.
ASTRAL NUMBER, 12772.

MERCURY.

Sudden illness or an accident. Injury to some person. A bitter disappointment, but one that will soon pass. Dissatisfaction with labor.

VENUS.

Illness caused by powerful emotions. Illness of a lady friend, or relative by marriage. A disappointment of a wish or aspiration to succeed.

MARS.

A lawsuit. Disappointment caused by a man. Ill success in some undertaking. Loss caused through illness. In some cases a secret disclosure.

JUPITER.

Financial loss, disappointment, trouble, failure, bankruptcy, default of employee and kindred troubles, according to other indications in same lay-out.

SATURN.

An illness of self, or a near friend. If with 7 s, it indicates a fatal termination. If near your birth card, it warns you to be extremely careful of yourself.

URANUS.

Disappointment in one's labor. A disagreeable labor performed. A disappointing occurrence at a distance. A missed opportunity. Disappointment in a real estate deal.

NEPTUNE.

An accident by water. Illness caused by dampness. Disappointment regarding a journey. Bad news from a distance.

The Mystic Test Book.

GRAND SPREAD,
SOLAR.

——o——

FUTURE.

QUADRATED TO
TIME.

——o——

PAST.

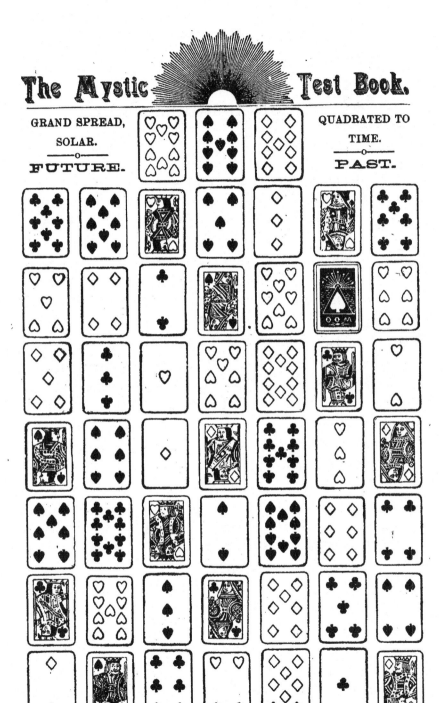

SOLAR VALUE,   49.

SPIRIT VALUE   45.

ASTRAL NUMBER, 65413.

MERCURY.

Successful labor. A quick return for labor performed. Professional success. Success in a speculation. Success in a business connected with rapid transportation.

VENUS.

Success and happiness in one's labor, home life and general surroundings. Indications especially strong for females. Success in business where females are largely employed.

MARS.

Strength to bear trouble and to labor for some great good. General success, especially for males. In some cases predicts success in a lawsuit.

JUPITER.

General pecuniary success in mercantile pursuits, professional undertakings, and manufacturing enterprises. A strong card under Jupiter.

SATURN.

Success in the practice of medicine, healing and kindred pursuits. Indicates recovery from illness when such is shown elsewhere. Counteracts the nine of spades.

URANUS.

Good and increasing success in all pursuits connected with labor. Success in real estate transactions. Overcoming of troubles.

NEPTUNE.

Success in pursuit of various kinds connected with travel, especially with the water. Fishing, boating and travel by water.

The Mystic Test Book.

GRAND SPREAD,
SOLAR.

FUTURE.

QUADRATED TO
TIME.

PAST.

SOLAR VALUE,　　50.

SPIRIT VALUE,　　55.

ASTRAL NUMBER, 26666.

MERCURY.

An industrious young man.　A man who is engaged in some line of work requiring quickness and skill.　A successful man in most cases.

VENUS.

An industrious man who is engaged in some occupation that is clean and light, requiring keen perceptions and ability to make and keep friends.

MARS.

A gentleman connected with the law. or some trade requiring strong will force and power, or, in some cases, manly strength.

JUPITER.

An active young man, engaged in some mercantile or professional pursuit.　A powerful worker.　Steady and industrious.

SATURN.

A young or middle aged man engaged in some pursuit connected with medicine, such as a physician, druggist, or something of the kind.

URANUS.

A hard-working young or middle aged man.　In some cases a dealer in real estate.　In some aspects indicates a farmer or laborer.

NEPTUNE.

Usually indicates a sailor, or one connected with water transportation; but may also represent a traveling salesman or tradesman.

The Mystic Test Book.

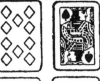

SOLAR VALUE, 51.

SPIRIT VALUE, 65.

ASTRAL NUMBER, 44576.

MERCURY.

An industrious lady, who is quick of motion and hurries about her work. Generally quite nervous in temperament.

VENUS.

An affectionate, faithful and industrious wife and mother. In some cases, however, it indicates a single lady of same disposition.

MARS.

A hard-working woman, inclined to a masculine bearing. Sometimes shows a quarrelsome woman and one who talks against her neighbors.

JUPITER.

A business lady. One who loves to transact business and to handle money. In some cases one who is employed in a mercantile institution.

SATURN.

Sometimes indicates a female physician. A lady who is ill. A lady employed in some place where the sick are treated.

URANUS.

A hard-working woman, who delights in running things. She cannot bear to see a speck of dirt about the house. Kindly disposition.

NEPTUNE.

A lady who is a worker in some line affecting or connected with travel. In some cases the wife of a man who travels. A traveled lady, a worker.

The Mystic Test Book,

GRAND SPREAD,
SOLAR.

———o———

FUTURE.

QUADRATED TO
· TIME.

———o———

PAST.

SOLAR VALUE, 52.
SPIRIT VALUE, 75.
ASTRAL NUMBER, 44585.

MERCURY.

A quick-tempered, hard-working, rushing man. One who employes many workmen, in some cases. An energetic business man

VENUS.

A man of kindly disposition, not very wealthy, usually one who is a hard worker. Kind to his family. In some cases the head of a concern employing females.

MARS.

Usually denotes an industrious, professional gentleman. An attorney at law, a judge, or some office holder. In some cases, the head of a concern employing male help.

JUPITER.

A manufacturer or a gentleman who employs a great deal of labor. A self-made man. A man of influence. A business rusher.

SATURN.

An old and experienced physician. In some cases a hard-worked man who has bad health. Usually represents an over-worked person.

URANUS.

A sober, industrious, business man who carries on a business that employs others. A controller of labor. A real estate dealer.

NEPTUNE.

A gentleman connected with travel and taansportation. In some cases an officer, a captain of a vessel or a superintendent of some company employed in water traffic.

The Mystic Test Book.

GRAND SPREAD, SOLAR.				QUADRATED TO TIME.

FUTURE. —o—   PAST.

CHAPTER VIII.

The Solar Quadrate.

THE CROSS OF CHRIST. FURTHER INSTRUCTION IN
DELINEATING.

N page 58 we gave an "Independent Solar
Spread," which is explained upon page 57.
Now, there are many strange properties connected with this solar spread, or quadrate from
the solar test book. We have explained on
pages 45 to 47 some of these properties, but we
will give here something more. On page 181 we give the
"Grand Cross," which represents the Cross of Christ, with
Jesus, the Teacher of Nazareth, upon the center of the
cross, represented by the emblem which in mystic language
indicates a single man with a kind and loving heart, ruling under Venus. But in the solar test book he comes
in the same place in all its quadrations.

The two Marys are seen at the foot of the cross, the

The Mystic Test Book.

Grand   Cross

secret emblem at the top with the emblems of power on each side. The eight at the right hand end of the cross represents power in knowledge. I will not give all the emblematic meanings here, leaving much for our mystic friends to study out.

But we will call the attention of the student to the fact that the quadration from the solar test book, endlessly produces Christ *upon the same place in this cross.* The king of spades, a representative of the kingly power, and the 8 of clubs before spoken of, remain throughout all the quadrates in the same positions. The king at the head of the sun line. In order to illustrate this fully, and at the same time to give our readers the first 12 solar quadrates complete, we will give upon the next alternating pages from 183 to 203 inclusive, the other eleven solar quadratic spreads. They are all well worthy of study as independent quadrates.

Following this series, we will give upon pages 205, 207 and 209 samples of quadrated astral test book, upon astronomical time, with the deal in fours. There are thousands of these, so we give only three for purposes of study. With this explanation, we are prepared to go on with our work.

FARTHER EXPLANATIONS OF DELINEATING.

Combinations of cards, either under one planet or side by side in same life lines, change the indications very materially. That is, combinations tending in a certain direction, either good or bad, favorable or unfavorable, are stronger than the indications of their component parts would be if in separated positions.

The Mystic Test Book.

GRAND SPREAD,
SOLAR.
—o—
FUTURE.

QUADRATED TO
TIME.
—o—
PAST.

For instance, take the following:

This combination indicates that the person will gain many friends and through that power he will have the power of gaining wealth; that he will have great success in applying his knowledge to business matters and he will succeed in making money. The two tens not only double the effect by being together, but show a blending influence in the shape of a double success in wealth and knowledge.

The same is true of all doubles, and three or four cards of same spot value, together, increase the power in like proportion.

On the other hand take the following:

     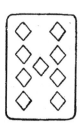

This combination is a very bad one and indicates trouble, worry, illness, loss of a friend, loss of money or property, disappointment in labor and in business, and a double disappointment besides.

NEUTRALIZING INFLUENCES.

When cards of opposing qualities come together they neutralize each other in such a manner that the full meaning of each cannot be taken.

GRAND SPREAD,
SOLAR.
—o—
FUTURE.

QUADRATED TO
TIME.
—o—
PAST.

In this illustration the five of spades, indicating a change or a journey, is contra-indicated by the six, which shows that the change or journey contemplated will be postponed for a time. This will cause a disappointment, but the ten of hearts following the nine, or by its side, indicates that the disappointment will be slight. The trouble with some money matter, shown by the seven of diamonds, is only partially neutralized by the ten, because the suit is different·

THE GENERAL RULE.

Emblems of the same suit, that indicate opposite, or nearly opposite, qualities, strongly neutralize each other.

If the suits are different they only partly neutralize each other.

PLANETARY NEUTRALIZATIONS.

When a good card comes under a bad planet, or a bad card comes under a good planet, the indications are neutralized to a certain extent, dependant upon the surroundings. As an illustration take the following:

VENUS.

The Mystic Test Book.

**GRAND SPREAD,
SOLAR.**

———o———

FUTURE.

**QUADRATED TO
TIME.**

———o———

PAST.

Here the seven of hearts is neutralized in its effect by ruling under Venus, and so also is the nine of clubs. The four of hearts is augmented by its position, while the ten of diamonds is slightly lowered in its power, because Venus is antagonistic to Jupiter, the principal ruler in diamonds.

In short, the student should constantly bear in mind the suits ruling naturally under each planet and give due force to the changes produced by emblems appearing under different aspects.

These various changes in indications are provided for as far as possible in the tables of indications preceding, but the almost infinite combinations and meanings cannot all be provided for.

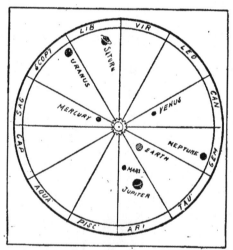

POSITION OF THE PLANETS AT THE TIME.

The professional expert, who wishes naturally to give as perfect a delineation as possible, will need a "trestle-board" upon the wall, exhibiting the planets in their proper positions for the time.

The Mystic Test Book.

GRAND SPREAD,
SOLAR.

QUADRATED TO
TIME.

FUTURE.

PAST.

❧The Planets, Earth and Moon.❧

For the benefit of numerous students of astralism who have the necessary knowledge and means of tracing these bodies in their revolution about the sun we give a very brief synopsis of their characteristic effects.

Planet of impulse. Passion, sex love, activity, sudden changes. Stimulator of magnetism. Accidents. Quickener of effects of other planets. Rules fevers and all inflammatory diseases.　**H**

Planet of love. Beauty, purity, devotion, harmony, ideality, spirituality, affection, esteem, kindness, blandness, music, poetry, art, grace, connubial love, honor and truth. Rules emotional diseases.　**H**

Planet of war. Inharmony, quarrels, law suits, combativeness, antagonism, strength, vitality, sex force, restlessness under restraint. Rules liver and bilious diseases, headache and dyspepsia.　**C**

Planet of wealth. Power, avariciousness, pride, control, governing force, greatness, elegance, order, ascendancy, love of money, strength of will, selfish instinct, memory of events, firmness. Rules appoplexy and many diseases of the brain.　**D**

Planet of inharmony. Sickness, death, enmity, anger, selfishness, intoxication, gluttony, poverty, disgrace, ill luck, hardship. Rules diseases of all kinds, in each house of the Zodiac.　**S**

Planet of Labor. Domesticity, love of nature and the young, life force high, veneration. justice, foresight, frugality, ingenuity. Appertains to the ground. Rules weakness and all diseases caused by a low vibratory force.　**S**

Planet of water. Locality, or power to remember places, bibativeness, sailing, traveling, sublimity or love of the marvelous, intuition, application, eventuality, self control. Rules rheumatism and all diseases made worse by dampness.　**D**

MOON. Satellite of earth. Rules all forms of insanity and crankiness. Effect constant upon inhabitants of earth but varied by polar changes.　★

EARTH. Planet of selfishness. Grasping, greed, acquisitiveness, tyranny, love of money and power, effect constant upon the inhabitants thereof, but changed according to polarity of earth in the various houses.　**C**

The Mystic Test Book.

GRAND SPREAD,
SOLAR.
FUTURE.

QUADRATED TO
TIME.
PAST.

We keep a pamphlet for sale at the Grand Temple each year, which gives the position of the planets for the year. Sent postpaid for 25 cents, to any address. When certain planets are in strong aspect to each other; for instance in conjunction or opposition; or when two planets are each in the same aspect relative to the earth, such as quadrature or sextile; the emblems ruling *in the same life line* and under those co-ordinating planets *act together,* so as to augment their effect or neutralize each other in the same manner as when such appear together under one planet.

In order to aid the student in understanding the planetary effects, so that he can calculate as nearly as possible as to whether the effects co-ordinate, antagonize or are neutral in any given condition. We give a condensed, general table of planetary effects on page 190.

The letters at the side are the ones used to indicate the suits and are always used in recording the names of emblems, instead of writing the names out in full.

The earth and moon both act together and rule in clubs, but the card lay-outs do not spread cards for those bodies because the earthly and lunarian magnetism is already accounted for in the planetary calculations. The earth effect is a " constant," that is a force constantly acting at the same distance, upon the inhabitants.

The effects of the moon is nearly a constant as to *distance* but constitutes a changeable force as to polarity

While the brains of a human being are in a good normal state, Luna has but little effect upon that person except in the physical condition.

But the moment that the brain becomes diseased, the rate

The Mystic Test Book.

GRAND SPREAD,
SOLAR.

FUTURE.

QUADRATED TO
TIME.

PAST.

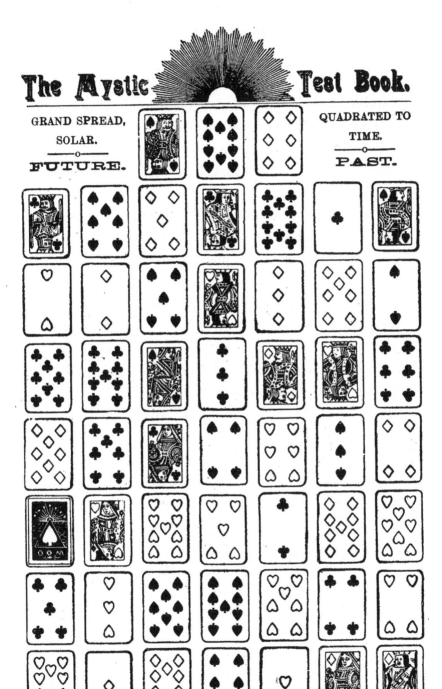

of psychic vibration comes within the power of the moon to co-ordinate therewith and just in proportion to the extent of the cerebral unbalancing or derangement the moon's effect takes the place of the normal planetary effects.

A WONDERFUL PECULIARITY.

It is a strange fact, but it has been determined by observations, that a lay-out of cards, spread from the handling and mixing of a lunatic, actually *become reversed* in their meanings and all rule under the moon. Bad cards are better than the normal indication, while good ones become bad.

Success becomes disappointment, love becomes hate, virtue and goodness become immorality and sin. Trouble and weakness are no longer indicated by sevens but by eights.

Predictions made regarding the action of insane persons, under given conditions, must be more or less reversed according to the extent of the mental aberation.

THE EFFECT INDICATED BY SUN CARDS.

There are always three cards called "sun cards" in each lay-out. These cards are the ones that do not rule under any one of the planets at the time, and they are usually regarded as emblems of effects that *are not in the person's life at the time.* By some masters, they are considered as events or conditions passed and gone out of the person's life.

From my own observations, I am inclined to the belief that the sun cards simply indicate that those conditions are *not at present in force* in the planetary aspects prevailing at the time.

Heliocentric astrology does not take the apparent motion of the sun into consideration, for the sun effect is always about the same and is called the "solar constant."

The Mystic Test Book.

GRAND SPREAD,
SOLAR.

——o——

FUTURE.

QUADRATED TO
TIME.

——o——

PAST.

THE EFFECT OF THE SUN.

But the manner in which this solar effect is received *by the earth* is very important and is fully considered in the calculations of polarity relative to the earth. These polar changes are all calculated on a time basis, for "time" is nothing but a measure of motion of the heavenly bodies, particularly the earth.

If the earth stood perpendicular to the plain of its revolution about the sun, the polar changes would be so slight as to scarcely be worth calculating, and if, at the same time, the orbit of the earth was perfectly circular and the inclination of the sun zero, there would be no change to calculate through polarity and it would make no possible difference when a person was born, whether it was in January or July.

The student will understand by this explanation that the "signs of the Zodiac" are nothing but points of measurement dividing the heavens into twelve portions and that these signs are only emblems and tokens of the twelve grand polarities of the earth as that body moves around Old Sol in his yearly journey.

The signs themselves have no magnetic effect whatever, the mass of suns in each sign being too numerous and too far away to be calculated or considered by mathematics.

MILLIONS OF YEARS HENCE.

After the lapse of an enormous time, comparatively speaking, the planet Jupiter will have cleared its atmosphere of its

The Mystic Test Book.

GRAND SPREAD,
SOLAR.

FUTURE.

QUADRATED TO
TIME.

PAST.

loads of carbon, and metalic vapors now held from its surface by the power of heat vibrations, and he will become the abode of human beings. There, under the ever present and ever acting laws of evolution those beings will arrive at a high state of civilization, growth and spiritual power.

At first they will be obliged to pass through the errors and follies incident to all early growths. The people will allow kings and self-appointed priests to rule over them. Human liberty will be trampled in the dust for ages and ages.

But the time will come when the "Religion of the Stars" will be the religion of Jupiter, and kings and priests will be no more forever on that planet.

There are many reasons for this prediction. One is that Jupiter is inclined but slightly to the plane of the ecliptic, which will make the seasons uniform and the effects from magnetic conditions very constant. While the enormous length of time that the planet will be in a condition to sustain life, will give ample scope for the work of evolution to advance the people to a high state of unfoldment.

But our business is with our own little insignificant speck of a planet, at present, so we will endeavor to not wander away again.

The Mystic Test Book.

CHAPTER IX

Tarotology.

THE WONDERFUL PROPERTIES OF THE TEST BOOK TAROTS.

HE strange properties of the Mystic Test Book are beautifully illustrated by means of the tarots made from its magic pages. The ancients called these tarots "Magic" squares or "Magi" squares, and they are found carved upon stone upon ancient monuments.

The squares thus found, however, are those made of ordinary numerals, because the ones made of the symbols of the Test Book are much more difficult to represent upon stone besides being held as too sacred to be thus made public.

But the sacred quality is looked upon quite from a different standpoint now. The Order regards the Test Book and all the other matters connected with our religion and work as "sacred," only in the sense that all knowledge is sacred.

The Mystic  Test Book.

GRAND SPREAD,
SOLAR.
——o——
FUTURE.

QUADRATED TO
-TIME.
——o——
PAST.

We no longer look upon anything with that superstitious reverence that belongs to the childhood of races, when men saw a God or demon in everything that was the least bit out of the common.

It will be impossible, in this work, to give a full and comprehensive treatise upon the subject, that will enable the student to find individual tarots for any and all birth dates, because the key birth tarots alone, from which the test book tarot sare constructed, number six thousand eight hundred and sixteen.

The key tarots from which these 6,816 are constructed, number six hundred and forty-four, and they are only to be found in two books upon this planet. Therefore we only intend to give, in this work, elementary instruction upon a subject that is practically infinite in extent.

The simplest form of tarot known is the 3x3 number tarot.

$$\begin{array}{ccc} 8 & 1 & 6 \\ 3 & 5 & 7 \\ 4 & 9 & 2 \end{array}$$

The horizontal lines, perpendicular lines and the diagonals from corner to corner each add up 15, which is equal to the figures in one row multiplied by the center figure, five.

In all odd numbered magic squares this law holds good.

We will now produce the same from leaves of the Mystic Test Book.

The spot value of the emblems, being the same as in the

The Mystic Test Book.

| GRAND SPREAD, SOLAR. | | | | QUADRATED TO TIME. |

FUTURE.   **PAST.**

number tarot, forms a perfect tarot as in the preceding, but

in addition we find that the solar values of the cards form
the following tarot:

34 1 19

3 18 33

17 35 2

This is "perfect," because all the eight lines add up 54.
That is it is a perfect solar tarot, or physical tarot. But it
is not a perfect spirit tarot in any manner whatsoever, for
the first line at the left adds up 184, the next perpendicular
line 95 and the last 54. The spirit results are mixed.

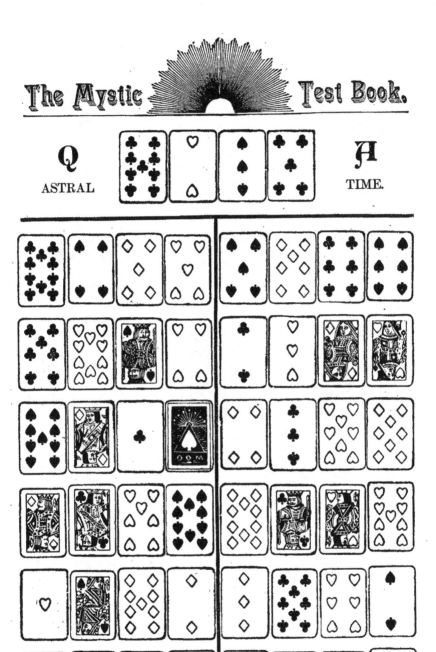

Q ASTRAL ... A TIME.

Let us take another one now and note the difference.

THE SPOT VALUE.

12	5	10
7	9	11
8	13	6

THE SOLAR VALUE

38	5	23
7	22	37
21	39	6

The first forming a perfect tarot adding up 27, or 3 times 9.
The second being a perfect tarot adding up 66, or 3 times 22.

Now take the spirit values of the same cards, found below.

This is a perfect "spirit tarot" adding up one hundred and twenty-six on all its eight lines. That is, three times 42, its central number.

Q

ASTRAL

A

TIME.

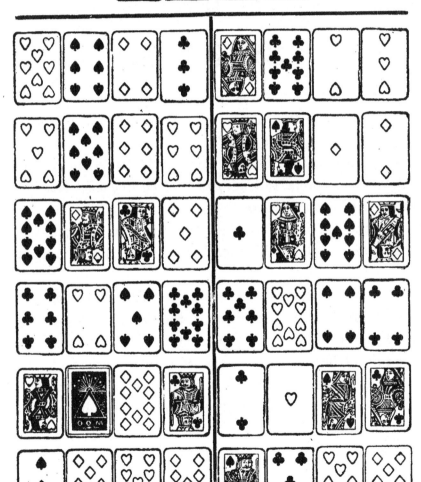

Why is it, think you, that the same tarot of cards, when made of different emblems, changes its properties? If one or more have this property, why not all?

24 50 52

70 42 14

32 34 60

Again, when we find the spirit of these cards so completely different from the solar values and spot values, *why should they ever form a perfect tarot?*

The reason is this, because these cards have divine properties, or occult properties *not possessed by any other book that ever existed upon our planet.*

For the purpose of further illustration of this point we will again produce the sacred star and examine into its properties.

The tarot in the center shows the emblems of wisdom, running from the quarter of labor to the quarter of knowledge.

The queen of love rules upon the point of the star where the four of hearts represents satisfaction in love and friendship. The knave of hearts is in the point of "power in love" and his position corresponds to the male birth house, that is, Aries.

The king of hearts is in the place of marriage, that is, the house of Gemini.

Upon the points, the seven of hearts, with the double signification, spiritually good; physically bad; rules with Leo,

Q

ASTRAL

A

TIME.

the emblem of the Infinite Power, and Cancer, the emblem
of the retrogression of the physical.

The ace of spades, the *secret emblem*, representative of the
secret order, stands between the balances of Libra, and the
Virgin of the sixth house upon one of the dark or " occult "
points of the star.

The 2 of spades on another dark point represents " union
in labor."

All the points from the Magi card around to the left, form the *sacred number* that we gave on page 23 in the emblems of wisdom, which represents one-seventh of the number of the Infinite.

The spot value of this row is just equal to 3 times 9, or 27, the same number that constitutes *the sum of each row in the central tarot.* But the solar values add up 144, the occult number 12x12 used so much in the mystic books of the Bible.

But, now observe the vast difference between the spirit values of the sacred number and the tarot. While the former$=44+40+54+80+84+70$, which equal 372 or 12 times 31, the latter, or tarot lines are but 126.

TAROT SOLAR VALUES	TAROT SPIRIT VALUES.
12 33 21	31 63 32
31 22 13	43 42 41
23 11 32	52 21 53

The solar values add 66 against 144 on the points, *while the spot values are the same.* Again, take the cards on any two opposite points, light plus dark, positive and negative, and they invariably add up the same on all the points, thus we find that as different as the various values are, the co-ordinations are so perfect that each opposite pair of points

The Mystic Test Book.

TAROT   SPECIAL

balance with eacn of the others as shown in the following table:

Quarter values add up   5
Spot values add up   9
Suit values add up   39
Solar values add up   48
Spirit values add up   124

The three triangles together$=$12 times 31$=$372.

We wish to particularly impress upon the minds of our readers the fact that these numbers are not like mere words which are arbitrary and invented by human beings, but on the contrary, these wonderful and astonishing mathematical relations, connected with the Test Book, are *divine attributes inherent in the very laws of the Infinite.* Therefore they are fixed facts, not only upon this particular earth; but upon all the planets that exist throughout the vast realms of space.

THE SIXTEEN MAGIC TAROT.

The next tarot to the one we have been considering, and by far the most important, is the one containing sixteen squares or 4 times 4.

These are called "birth tarots," from the fact that every person born into the world has one as his or her ruling tarot.

In all, there are many millions of these tarots, and the one belonging to any individual can only be found by a mathematical calculation.

Some person's tarots are perfect in spirit as well as the solar values. Others are very imperfect, while some are partly perfect in spirit and in some cases almost wholly so. The tarot of any person shows how well the astral or spirit is balanced to the mentality and physical.

In some the solar values are low, while the spirit values are high. In others the law is reversed. But the strangest peculiarity of all is, that some of the cards have *minus spirits* or what is called "double astrals," while there are persons to correspond.

It is not generally known that there are, here and there, persons who actually have a double inner self or astral and that one is positive, the other negative. I hesitate to put forth such facts without going into details which support the claim, but I will be obliged to only give the mathematical side of the question in this work, or the relations of the tarot to man.

RULE FOR FINDING THE NEGATIVE SPIRIT OF A CARD.

"*Subtract the positive spirit of the card from the number eighty-nine, and give the remainder the minus sign.*"

EXAMPLES OF DOUBLE ASTRALS.

Five of spades: positive 84, negative - 5
Seven of hearts: positive 70, negative 19
Nine of diamonds: positive 83, negative 6
King of clubs: positive 82, negative 7

As a matter of fact every card has a negative astral, and I am even inclined to believe that each and every human being has a negative spirit that comes uppermost under certain conditions, but the negatives of nearly all the cards do not appear to assert themselves only under very extraordinary circumstances.

In the same manner, the negative spirit of human beings generally keeps back, except in the case of some certain ones who appear, at least from a mathematical standpoint, to act under the negative astral nearly all the time. I have found several persons during our temple work of the past three years, *who act under the negative magnetic astral number* and calculations must be made accordingly in their cases.   This extends to planetary affects too.

The "Strange Case of Dr. Jekyl and Mr. Hyde," although written as a novel only, seems to be founded upon a fact in human nature.

The following examples of birth tarots are all taken from the Test Book at one time and they illustrate the various phases mentioned heretofore.

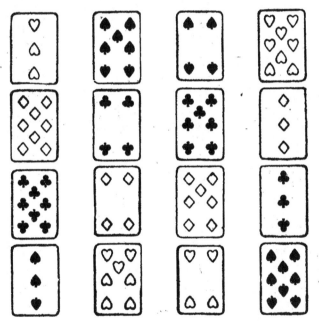

THE "CENTURY" TAROT.

One line of tarots, comprising 354,433 in number, are called "Century tarots," from the fact that their solar values add up just 100 on all the lines.   But they are also wonderful examples of high spirit tarots, the astrals adding

199 *on all lines,* thus showing them to be *perfect in spirit on the positive astrals.*

THE SOLAR VALUE.	THE SPIRIT VALUE
3 46 43 8	30 15 74 80
34 17 20 29	73 81 22 23
21 30 33 16	32 33 63 71
42 7 4 47	64 70 40 25
Adds 100.	Adds 199.

This line of tarots has a spirit value almost double the solar value. Lack but a unit.

EXAMPLE OF A SOLAR 122 TAROT FROM THE SAME BOOK.

Class 122, spot values add 44: solar values add 122: spirit values add 152; or exactly the Test Book number 52+100, the solar value of its mate given above. There are 54,528 of these tarots.

SPIRIT VALUES, SHOWING ONE NEGATIVE ASTRAL.

1 65 45 41

34 52 72 −6

82 4 24 42

35 31 11 75

In adding the lines, you should add the positives

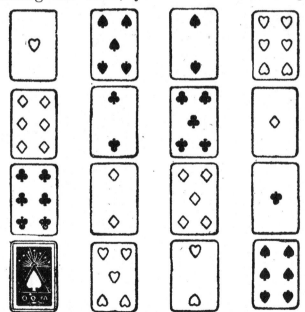

TAROT FROM CLASS NUMBER 92 SOLAR, FROM SAME BOOK.

together and subtract the negative from the sum. In this instance the negative used is that of the nine of diamonds. 75+42+41=158. 158—6=152. The cross line adds in same manner 152. In class 92 the spirits are perfect, adding 119, but using the negative spirit of the 5 of spades which is—5. This series contains 27,564 tarots. This entire "book," which means 48 cards, 4x12, exclusive of the knaves, contains 436,224 tarots.

TAROT FROM CLASS NUMBER 96 SOLAR: SERIES 842.

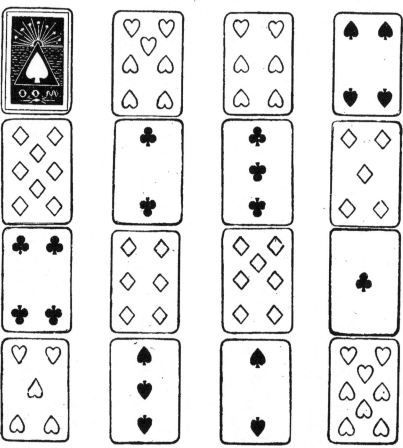

Another series is still more remarkable for the wide

divergence between the solar and spirit values, also from the fact that the astrals are all positive and perfect. This is class 96, number of tarots 109,056. Entire series 272,448. Spirits add up 248; *more than two and one-half times the solar values.*

One peculiar series are called "Court Tarots" from the fact that they are composed of all the court cards.

EXAMPLE OF SOLAR COURT TAROTS NUMBER 124.

Up to the present time but 27,264 are known of the class number 124, but it is quite probable that this will be exceded. It belongs to a very large series, containing nearly half a million in number.

The solar values and spirit values of class 124 are very nearly balanced, 124 to 172.

NAMES OF THE FIVE "POINTS" OF A TAROT.

All tarots, of whatever number of squares, have five points, consisting of the four corners and the center. In odd numbered tarots, such as 9 or 25 square, the center square is one of the "points." But in even square tarots such as the 16 or 36, the center point is where the middle lines cross.

The names of these points are as follows, being the ones used in ancient times:

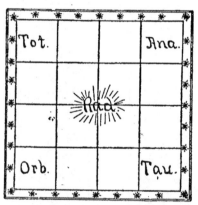

The word "Tot" means small, and denotes the place of the Ego or 1, in a tarot of first position. "Ana" signifies "over, opposite to another." "Rad" signifies a root or center from which points radiate. "Orb" means the earth, and that corner is ruled by the earth in the male line of a 16 tarot.

Tau" signifies "over, beyond, to a point beyond another."

HOW TAROT SQUARES COME UNDER THE PLANETS.

The male squares in a tarot are those forming a " Saint

Anthony Cross," or the letter **X**, and the planets rule as follows therein:

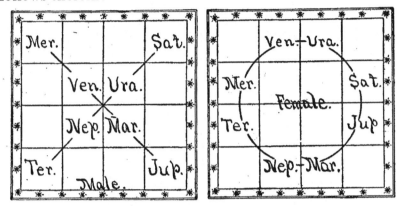

The female squares of a tarot fill the remaining squares and form a circle.

THE FEMALE CIRCLE OF PLANETS.

This line differs somewhat from the former conceptions held regarding the female squares. Later discoveries changing the rulings on some squares.

We see here illustrated the very original conception of the cross **X**, and circle ◯, as emblems of sex.

Any tarot can be changed or transposed from a Mercury tarot to that of any other planet, by crossing the cards over uniformly in such a manner as to bring the *place of the Ego to the square ruled by the planet*; but this change revolves the ego in the female circle constantly, if the tarot is a feminine tarot, and on the contrary the ego remains in the **X**, if the tarot is a male one.

If the changes are made in such a manner as to throw the ego from the ◯ to the **X**, or *vice versa*, the tarot will be changed in its entire nature and in many cases rendered an imperfect one. At the least it will be thrown into another series or class, very different from its former solar rank.

The following series of seven cuts, exhibits in a graphic manner the way changes are made from the primary, or

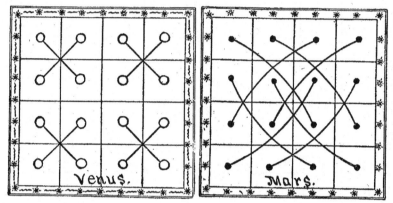

Mercury tarot, to each of the other planets. The lines drawn from one dot to another, signify that the emblems or figures in those squares are to be exchanged one with another

In the illustration of Jupiter the crossing from corner to corner is indicated by arrows to save the confusion of lines.

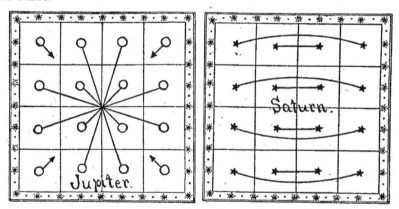

Any sixteen tarot that exists, can be changed thus, without spoiling its characteristics.

There are many other changes that could be shown upon diagrams, illustrating the movement of the numbers, in changing from series to series and class to class, but it is

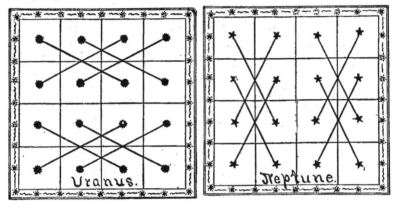

not intended to give a complete description of all the complex changes that are made in this branch of occult symbolism, because the reader could not well understand it anyway. Besides this he could not carry on the calculations

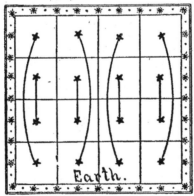

without the elaborate keys and tables necessary,

Should my time permit, I intend to get out a special work on tarotology, with all the key tarots, tables and directions, some time in the future. Such a work will require much time and labor.

In an impersonal card tarot, the " ego square " is always the one which is occupied by the card having the smallest solar value.

But in a *personal* tarot, the square occupied by the birth card of the person, is called the " Ego Square."

The following tarot, class 158 solar, is very remarkable from the fact that the spirit and solar values are so nearly alike. The solar value, 158, being actually greater than the spirit value, which is but 156.

MERCURY TAROT, CLASS 158, SERIES 621.

Class 158 is entirely in diamonds and spades, but the other classes in same series are in other suits and are devoid of the peculiarity mentioned.

Class 158 contains 13,632 tarots. One class belonging to series 621 is somewhat remarkable for just the opposite quality, as its spirit is more than three times its solar value.

There are other members of this series that are peculiar in various directions.   One of the tarots in another class is given below as a sample from same series.

A MARS MALE TAROT, CLASS 54, SERIES 136.

Solar value 54: spirit value 184: number of tarots, 13,632.

Strange to say, every class and series have their peculiarities in the same way that people and animals have theirs.   Yet, like animals, and even vegetables, there is a law that runs through all, that is manifest to us upon examination in a certain geometrical form that exists with all tarots.

We will next give an example of a large class of tarots that belong in solar 96, same class as the one given a few pages back, that has a constant spirit of 248, positive. But, strange to say, this one, although of same solar class, is not spiritually perfect at all; some lines adding 70, some

248 and some 159. There are a large number of " off spirit " tarots, there being no less than *a hundred thousand in one series*. Persons who are born under the rulings of one of these species, are of changeable, mixed astral development and cannot be taught spiritual things scarcely at all.

SATURN, FEMALE TAROT, CLASS 108. SERIES 136.

Solar 108: spirit 142: number in class 27,264.

But there is a wide diversity in even the component members of the same class, for some of them are nearly perfect in spirit and some can be made perfect by one or two negatives.

Another peculiar thing about this particular class of tarots is the fact that a transformation from one planet to another often changes certain squares to negatives and at the same time changes negatives to positives. In other words, *the changes of the environment of the tarot changes its spiritual nature.* Other tarots, given heretefore, do not change in spirit under environment.

MERCURY MALE TAROT FROM CLASS 96, SERIES 268.

This would seem to be in perfect harmony with human nature, as we understand it, for we often see people who correspond to these two classes of tarots. One class always remaining uniform in spiritual growth as well as in the inner life; the other class changing under environment, in spirit and life, so to be scarcely recognized as belonging to the same class.

By the use of the negative of the 3 of spades the horizontal and perpendicular lines are brought to 159, but the cross lines **X** are each 248 and *cannot be changed by negatives.*

SAMPLE FROM CLASS 96, SERIES 268.

This is a sample of the " off spirit " class, in second and third quarter emblems. It has no less than three expressions of spirits, like its male mate above, in same class.

CHAPTER X.

The Tarot and the Zodiac.

WHY THE SIXTEEN SQUARE TAROTS ARE BIRTH TAROTS.
CALCULATIONS REGARDING THEM.

HE reason why the 4x4 tarots are considered as birth tarots, are many. We will give a few of them here, so that the reader can comprehend in a measure what lies beyond our ordinary grasp.

In the first place, anything that is used by workers in the occult line, should have within itself conformity to the motions of the heavenly bodies and time. Time is only an abstract, however, and does not really exist, for we can have no conception of time only as it measures the motion of something we are familiar with.

Thus we say "day" to express the fact that the earth has revolved once upon its axis. We say "year," as a convenient way of stating that the earth has performed a revolution about the sun. Of course we can divide and sub-divide these expressions for convenience sake; but all fractions partake of the same quality as the whole.

We have shown how the Test Book conforms to time, which is really motion, so we will now show how the sixteen tarot conforms to time and motion.

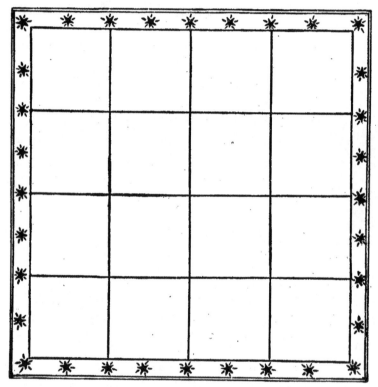

ILLUSTRATION OF A 4x4 TAROT FRAME.

The tarot frame given here will be an excellent place for the owner of this book to enter his own mathematical tarot when he becomes possessed of it, thereby having it for purpose of study and permanent record.

The perpendicular, middle line, is the celestial meridian; the horizontal line that crosses it midway, is the line of the

Apsides, both lines corresponding to the same ones used on the celestial sphere or the Zodiac. These lines, called the "Celestial Cross," (+) divide the tarot into four grand quarters, corresponding to the four seasons and the four quarters of the Zodiac, as well as the four chapters of the Test Book.

Beginning at the lower celestial meridian the houses of the Zodiac run around the outside in regular order as shown in cut.

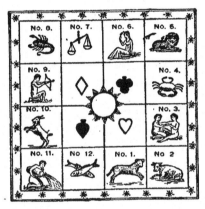

SIGNS OF THE ZODIAC ON TAROT.

The central part is the "*place of the sun*," and represents power and glory in the ancient symbolism. It too, is divided into four quarters, so that the tarot really expresses, not only the twelve houses of the Zodiac, but the four quarters at the same time.

The seven planets and the earth constitute with their satellites eight grand centers of vibratory force, or astral magnetism, in our solar system. The 4x4 tarot with its circle of planets in the female line and its cross, X, in the male line, represents them in their two-fold qualities, corresponding to the positive and negative in nature.

Birth tarot No. 1, mathematical, is formed from the numbers one to sixteen joined together under a certain law to form a complete and perfect tarot.

From this original Mercury tarot all the six thousand eight hundred and sixteen mathematical 4x4 birth tarots are constructed.

FORMATION OF TAROT NUMBER ONE.

Begin at the upper left hand corner of the tarot frame and enter the numbers in regular order from left to right, but *only those which fall in the male cross*

Secondly, begin at the lower right hand corner and enter the numbers in the same manner from right to left, except that you only enter them in the vacant female circle

1   15   14   **4**

12   **6**   **7**   9

8   **10**   **11**   5

13   3   2   **16**

We illustrate the tarot thus produced, showing the male numbers in black faced figures, the female in light. From this basic tarot all the Test Book tarots can be made.

Every perfect mathematical 16 tarot has the following peculiar properties:

1. The characteristic number, found by addition, is 34. which is composed of 3 and 4, which, in turn, add 7, the sacred number.

2. Every perpendicular and horizontal line, 8 in number add up 34 each.

3. The diagonal lines each add up 34.

4. The four sun squares in the center add just 34.

5. The four corner squares add exactly 34.

6. The two middle top squares + the two middle bottom squares equal 34.

7. The side squares, corresponding to the last, add up 34.

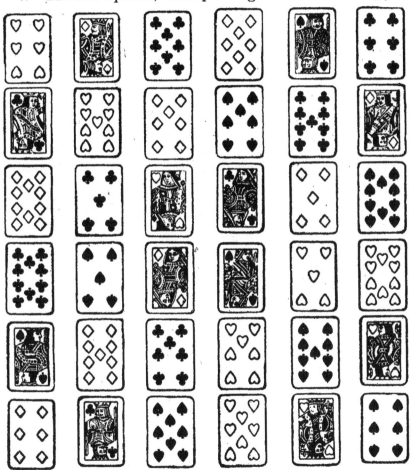

THE WONDERFUL 36 TAROTS.   THE "QUEEN" TAROT.

Many millions of these tarots are very beautiful and regular in form, and they are all interesting. The solar value of the Queen tarot is 171, spirit value 286, spot value 54, suit value 117, quarter value 15. All making perfect tarots when placed in frames by themselves.

The numbers of these tarots are simply beyond the human comprehension. It can be demonstrated by mathematics that a certain number of them could be constructed, but the number is so great that they never can be all constructed. They have the same peculiar properties belonging to the other tarots, only the powers are greatly enhanced from the fact that a 6x6 tarot combines the properties of the 9 and 16 tarots together.

Thus, we can form a 36 tarot by combining four 3x3 tarots in a proper manner, or we can make one by means of the tarot frame of card emblems as shown in the engraving.

The following cut exhibits a 36 tarot " frame " for holding a 4x4 tarot. The one shown belongs to the " Century tarots." In the vacant square we produce an engraving which will be found useful to the student of phrenology and astrology combined, but we will not enter into an explanation here. It speaks for itself however.

Any one of the millions of century tarots will fit into the inside of this frame and form a perfect 36 tarot, provided the 16 tarots are made of cards not in the frame. But millions of these frames can be formed, fitting around all sorts and classes of 16 tarots, making the permutations enormous.

One brother, who makes a study of 36 tarots, said: " The number that can be made of them, is like the sands of the sea for multitude."

Let us see if this is an exaggeration. One pound of fine sand contains about 700,000 "grains," or particles of sand, as found by counting and computation some years since.

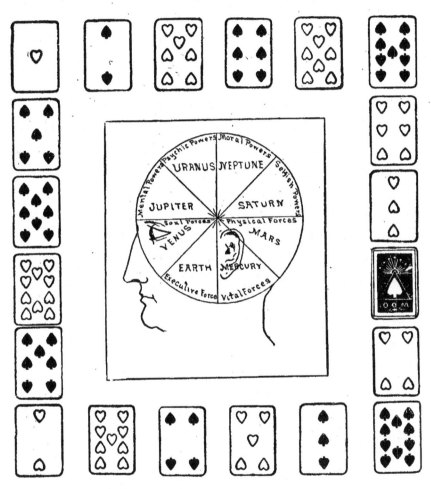

6x6 FRAME FOR CENTURY TAROTS.

One ton contains, on that basis, fourteen billion grains.

Our earth would contain, provided its immense bulk was all made of sand, 84,966 *septillions* of grains.

But the number of 36 tarots that can be constructed from

the Mystic Test Book is equal to the *thirty-second permuta-tion*, which is exactly:

263,130,836,933,693,530,167,218,012,160,000,000

or to express it in words, more than *two hundred and sixty-three thousand millions of septillions.* Therefore we are forced to the conclusion that the number of these tarots possible, is actually more than equal to the particles of sand that would be contained in *three millions of such globes as our earth.*

If we look at it from another standpoint, we are none the less astonished, for we find that for all of the enormous number of perfect tarots, the number of ways that the Test Book can be placed in the squares, *without forming a tarot,* is so perfectly enormous, that the mind of man cannot encompass it. There being more than a billion non-tarots to one tarot.

I am aware that these figures will lay me open to criticism from superficial thinkers, as did my statement in " Religion of the Stars," relating to homeopathic attenuations. But, if any person wishes to take me up on my statement contained herein, let him be sure of his figures before hand.

Several persons wrote to me upon the subject of the "homeopathic statement " I made on page 128 of the Templ Lectures, where I said that the *thousandth potency of natrum muriaticum* contained less than a grain of salt to ten thousand tons of sugar of milk, and a grain of *that* triturated with a million tons more of the sugar.

Some contended that the statement was "wild and unten-able." To satisfy myself as to whether I did make a " wild " statement or a "mild " one, I began a careful math-ematical examination of the question. Friends, as I am a living man, *I did not dare publish the results.* I was utterly astounded at the truth when I found it.

Why, my statement was so much *under* the truth in regard to quantity, that, if one called my statement *one grain of sand,* the *truth* would fill the entire space covered by our cluster of over sixteen million suns; which is so large that it is estimated that light consumes fifteen thousand years in crossing from one side to the other. Not only this, but there would be enough sand left over to fill the same space *more than fourteen thousand times ! !*

CALCULATIONS OF POTENCIES.

This is as good a place as we shall have to introduce the rules for the calculations of potencies on the decimal system. The reason for introducing it here is for the purpose of showing the connection between the mystic star and the units of measure.

It has been found from many sources, that of the pyramid measure being a prolific one, that measures are not arbitrary, but are all based upon some fact in nature. It is not strange that the repetend that occupies the points of the double triangle, being as it is, a repetend of the sacred number seven, should have some such connection. The star is on page 25.

Let it be required, to find how many pounds of sugar of milk there would be, to one grain's weight of the drug, in a decimal trituration. Let P represent any required potency. Then $P-3=x$. Then begin on the top point of the star and set down the number of spots on each card, passing to the left on the star and making your figures to the right of the seven. *Keep this going until you have made as many figures as will be equal to x.*

This is a solution of the problem which is indeed a tedious one by ordinary mathematics. What is more, it is absolutely correct. Avoirdupois weight is used, as that is the one for large weights.

EXAMPLE FOR PRACTICE

How many pounds of sugar of milk would there be, to one grain of salt, in a potency of 20, of *natrum muriaticum?* Ans. 14,285,714,285,714,285 or over fourteen quadrillions.

RULE NUMBER II.

To find how many tons of a trituration would contain one gram of the drug. Subtract eight from the number of the potency, or $P-8=x$.

Begin at the 7 point and set down the figures as in rule 1 to the amount of x. This gives the answer in tons.

Example: How many tons of sugar of milk would contain a grain of the active principle, at the 32d trituration, or potency?

Ans. 714,285,714,285,714,285,714,285, or over seven hundred sextillions of tons.

The statement made by me in " Temple Lectures" was equivalent to less than 20 sextillions of tons, so that if I had said the thirty-second potency, instead of the *thousandth*, my statement would then have been far below the truth, or thirty-five times too small

I do not intend to throw a straw in the way of that practice, however. In fact, I am a full believer in it and have used none other in my family for years. But I do want to impress upon the minds of our readers the great truth that the unseen astral potencies are *stronger than the seen.* I firmly believe that the potency of high homeopathic dilutions and triturations are in reality *spirit potentials*, and therefore heal through spirit power. These are my conclusions; take them or leave them as you choose.

Our sun, together with all his planets and satellites, weigh less than two octillions of tons. Less than one-third of the sugar of milk in the 36th potency, containing one grain of drug. Our entire system of suns are estimated at sixteen and a half millions in number and would weigh about thirty three million octillions of tons at the average weight of our own solar system. This vast weight is less than the amount of the forty-third decimal trituration.

So many people fail to grasp the wonders of nature, through their inability to realize the cold facts revealed by mathematical demonstration. Such persons cannot understand the wonders of the Mystic Test Book and the tremendous co-ordinations that exist with its emblems.

Some think "chance" brings about the wonders, when the results cannot by any possibility be attributed to chance.

In the same way, many erronious opinions are held by in dividuals, which opinions would be dispelled by a little common sense resort to mathematics. I have had numbers of people take up some statement of mine, such as the one regarding the "curve of the earth's orbit," and show from their treatment of the subject that they knew nothing about the mathematical laws governing curves.

In view of all the foregoing facts, the reader need not wonder that the author regards the "Religion of the Stars" as the divine religion of man, and mathematical science as its priest and interpreter.

CHAPTER XI.

The Lost Word. Other Wonderful Figures.

E have glanced briefly at the wonderful Egyptian tarots, and we have but to finish our book with a few other exemplifications of the mathematical co-ordinations of the little Mystic Test Book.

We have already shown, in former pages, how the book fits the Zodiac; one particular arrangement being upon page 27.

Another arrangement is such that each suit is spread in its own quarter, and the spot values are just equal to the degrees in each house. The four aces appear at the four corners and indicate the four quarters by suits; hearts, clubs, diamonds and spades.

The illustration, on this page, shows the emblems in the twelve signs of the Zodiac. Twelve times thirty equals 360, the degrees in the circle.

So the Test Book not only represents the days in a year but the degrees of the celestial circle. The two outside cards

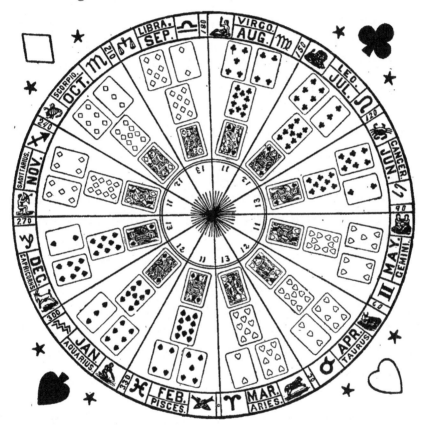

in each house add nine, the *golden number*, while the two inside ones add 21, that is, *three sevens*.

THE WORD OF ORIENTAL MYSTICISM.

"In the beginning was the word." That is, the long-lost word has its foundations in the very beginning of life, in the fundamental principles of nature.

Thousands and millions of human students of magic and occult knowledge, have searched for this word in vain. Thousands have claimed the possession of it, with no power or knowledge to back their pretentions.

Tho whole world *has the word*; the whole world *knows the word*; but few can *live the word*.

It is the most peculiar thing ever known on this planet. It is neither oblong, round nor square, yet it is a thing of beauty and "abideth with man for all earthly time."

It is two in one, it is three in one, and it is four in one. Its principles "abideth eternal in the heavens." It is of God, yet it is of man, for man, and by man.

The "word" must not only be lived in its component parts, but each and every mystic syllable and *even each letter* must be *lived* by the mystic who hopes to be able to use its wondrous power.

I am permitted by the higher brotherhood, to give one of the expressions of the "Word," the three, four and five expressed in mystic emblems, forming the sacred triangle:

It is generally known that all ancient secret orders both in Europe and Asia, regard this triangle as a significant portion of their teachings.

It is a basic, right-angled triangle, with its sides in such a proportion to each other that the smallest possible whole numbers can represent each of the sides. These numbers being *three, four* and *five*.

The sides of all right-angled triangles have the well known mathematical property, that the square of the base plus the square of the perpendicular, will equal the square of the hypotenuse.

To find numbers with these mathematical relations is not very easy, except by actual trial with figures. If you take the base, haphazard, and perpendicular also, when you come to square them and add them together, the chances are very great that no root can be found to the number produced by the addition.

For example, take for the base, 2, for the perpendicular, 3. The sum of their squares is equal to 13, therefore, the third side is equal to the square root of thirteen. There is no such number really in existence, in the universe.

1st. Any fraction, squared, must on pure mathematical principles produce a fractional number.

2d. Two whole numbers added must produce a whole number. Therefore a right triangle, such that the base and perpendicular each squared and added together forms a whole number, cannot have a hypotenuse *that can be found*, unless it be in whole numbers.

We know that the squares of 9 and 16 have for their roots 3 and 4, therefore 13 can have no whole number root. As we have shown heretofore, that a whole number cannot have a fractional root, because no fractional number in existence can be squared so as to produce a whole number, it follows that 13 *can have no numerical square root.* The root thereof is forever hidden from man.

Our readers may wonder why we introduce this explanation here. The reason is this, that those who are not practical, or even theoretical mathematicians, may thereby understand the wonders connected with the WORD in its relations to the emblems from the Magic Test Book. That they may fully understand that the wonderful co-ordinations that exist in the one phase given here, could not exist by any system of chance, by any arbitrary arrangement of the emblems, or by any species of occult necromancy known to human beings.

MYSTIC TRIANGLE OF THE MAGI.

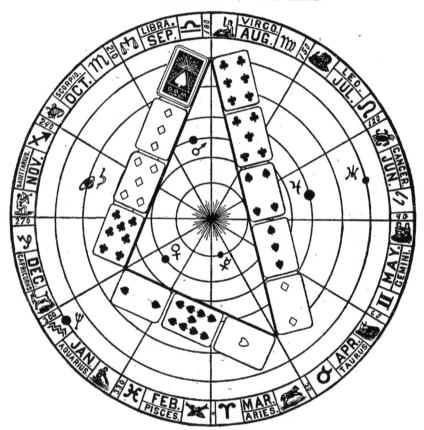

We will now explain the symbolism òf the mystic triangle, as spread upon a diagram of the celestial circle.

THE INNER AND OUTER. CIRCLES.

The inmost circle, or "Circle of Mercury," is drawn about the sun and just impinges upon the hypòtenuse of the triangle. The "Venus Circle" touches the perpendicular. The "Mars Circle" touches the base. That of Jupiter, the intersection of the base and perpendicular. "Saturn Circle" comes to the intersection of the base and hypotenuse. The "Circle of Uranus" strikes the third intersection. "Neptune Circle" encloses all and represents the outer darkness.

Thus we have the *six points* of this triangle represented, although the relative distances of the circles do not correspond to the physical distances of the orbits of the planets named. These circles all have fixed mathematical principles and proportions, wholly separate and apart from mere physical or concrete distance.

This being the case, the triangle can be conceived, of any dimension whatsoever and the one actually given has the same qualities both mathematical and geometrical, as one would have, that should extend from the orbit of Saturn on the second meridian to the orbit of Uranus, where it cuts the upper celestial meridian.

In fact, the same proportional triangle can be constructed so as to impinge at the points shown on the diagram, with the actual orbits of any two planets that may be selected at one time.

The triangle is shown in the illustration with the cards composing it placed so as to show the actual proportions 3: 4: 5, the cards thus forming by their *number*, the first or primary representation of the sides of the triangle.

The next co-ordination is shown from the Q values of the cards, which are as follows: Base, two spades=8, one heart=1, making 9. Perpendicular, one spade=4, two diamonds=6, one club=2, total 12. Hypotenuse, two spades=8, two clubs=4, one diamond=3, total 15. The square of 9+the square of 12 equals the square of 15. That is, 81+144=225.

Next construct the triangle from suit values, and to save space, we will use the initial letter of each of the names of the sides in place of the full name.

Suit values. B=39+39+0=78. P=39+26+26+ 13=104. H=78+26+26=130. Now we apply the test and we find that 78, 104 and 130 form a perfect triangle.

TRIANGLE FROM SOLAR VALUES.

B=1+48+41, total 90. P=20+31+29+40, total 120. H=19+18+43+42+28, total 150. Now we square these totals and find that the square of 90 plus that of 120, just equals the square of 150, which is 22,500. *Another perfect co-ordination.*

Remember what we have said about the difficulty of forming perfect triangles with perfect roots, and then consider the wonderful character of the above.

But this is not all, for another strange co-ordination exists. That is, that the sides of the solar value triangle *add up exactly 360, the degrees in the circle.* That is not all either, for the triangle covers the number of houses with each side that corresponds to the length of the sides and the solar values of each of these divisions *exactly equals the degrees in the houses covered.*

THE FINAL GRAND TEST.

All of the above is wonderful enough; but now we come to a higher and grander test still, one that is enough to almost take the breath away from a student of the occult, and to make him bow down in awe before the "little book" that possesses so many mysterious and divine attributes.

I confess that I should be afraid to give this final wonder, were it not that it is mathematically demonstrable, so that no skeptic can dispute it.

THE SPIRITS OF THE MYSTIC TRIANGLE.

Take the base. The spirit of the ace of hearts is 10, of the nine of spades 35, of the two of spades 54, a total of 99.

Take the perpendicular. The spirit of the seven of clubs is 22, of the five of diamonds 43, of the three of diamonds 23 and of the ace of spades 44, total 132.

Take the hypotenuse. The spirit of the two of diamonds is 13, of the three of spades 64, of the four of spades 74, of the five of clubs 2 and of the six of clubs 12, which together add up one hundred and sixty-five. Now, 99 squared= 9801. 132 squared=17424. 165 squared=27225. As 9801+ 17424=27225, *the numbers again represent a perfect triangle.*

The latter number represents the square of 15 in its 3 last figures, and 27, the 3 times 9, in its first two figures. The reader will remember the relations of these numbers in the 3x3 tarot heretofore given.

Aside from the overpowering proofs furnished by the absolute demonstration by mathematics, we notice many other peculiarities about the mystic triangle, which can be best appreciated by those persons who have made the journey "around the Zodiac."

For instance, it is "eternal in the heavens," inasmuch as it geometrically covers a given circle in the heavens in any and all cases. *It always did; it always will.* If every planet, as well as our sun, was annihilated, or turned to cold barren masses, the "WORD" would still, in the form of this grand triangle, cover its majestic sweep of the heavens; would still hold its mystic sway forever and ever.

We also notice in some minute particulars, such as the place of the Secret Magi emblem in the house of Libra that the cards themselves occupy emblematic places.

The nine of spades occupies the " house of death." The ace of hearts begins the quarter of love, with a heart single to the labor of love. From that house upward to the house of Virgo, each card corresponds in spot value to the house it occupies.

Coming down the line of the perpendicular, we have the one, three, five, seven, steps of the *Mystic Temple*. Add each spot value to that of its mate on the hypotenuse, beginning at the apex of the triangle, and we produce numbers which give the numbers of the house where the emblems are placed on the perpendicular line.

The sacred triangle is constantly showing itself in a multitude of ways in tarotology. It is truly wonderful to analyze card emblem tarots in all their manifestations under various conditions and to observe the peculiar triangular formations that manifest themselves.

On the next page we give the birth tarot of Mrs. L. J. Shafer, Grand Sentinel of the Temple at Chicago. We select this particular tarot for the reason that it exhibits several peculiar features, among which the " word " appears, exhibited in suits, in a variety of ways. It is a " mystic tarot " in every sense of the word.

The reader will first be apt to notice the row of mystic sevens running through the tarot. This is a peculiar feature and the strange part of it is, that in all this line, those four sevens stay together, sometimes running from corner to corner; again forming a group of four in the center of the tarot or in one corner. But they invariably appear in one of the sixteen characteristic positions which add 34 in the numerical birth tarot.

The one given is a Venus tarot; solar number 106, spirit 132, series 231, and the series contains 74,976 tarots.

THE TRIANGULAR FORMATION.

All through the tarot the right-angled triangle appears, both in suits and spot co-ordinates. For instance, the 7, 8 and 10 of spades as well as the 7, 8 and 9 form a triangle in each group. On close examination it will be observed that each suit forms in itself a counterpart of each of the others. So that what is true of one, is true of all. So we have eight perfect right-angled triangles, in suits, in this tarot.

Next we observe that the three sixes are in the form of a triangle on the right hand upper corner while the three eights balance them in a like triangle in the lower corner on the same side

SOLAR TAROT NO. 116, SERIES 861.

Strange to say, all through this series these two co-ordinating triangles keep their positions relative to each other except that they revolve at all angles and sometimes form larger triangles.

The number of tarots having the triangular peculiarity of

their suit arrangement is enormous. They appear in great numbers in the century series and likewise extend through all the other lines. Their exact number has not yet been computed, but it extends into millions.

We give a few isolated examples from various lines, on this and contiguous pages.

SOLAR TAROT NO. 112. SPOT VALUE 34.

Number 116 solar, illustrates a peculiar feature of certain lines of tarots. The reader will notice in different tarots, also in the tarot given on page 249, that the light suits form a peculiar shape which appears also reversed in the same shape in the light suits. The dark suits also form a counterpart, or negative to the light ones. Now, number 116 not only has this peculiarity in the suits, crossing the tarot horizontally, but it also shows the same identical form, in

court cards and common cards alternated, perpendicularly
As a curiosity, we will give a wonderful court tarot in nine
squares, that enjoys the distinction of being the most unique
of all tarots, inasmuch as but few of them exist. The same
is true also of one co-ordinating tarot in clubs, diamonds,
and spades, the only rival to the one given. The reader will

notice that the three Queens form one diagonal in order to
make the spot values 36, correct, while the other diagonal
contains the three clubs that are necessary to give the solar
and suit values. In no other way can a tarot be formed in
three suits.

On the following page we give a mystic chart that has
been in the archives of the Order for ages. It represents a magic square of words in the first square, where
the letters are so arranged that a number of the symbolic

words used by the Order are to be found in the readings up, down, across and diagonally. Like all other productions emanating from the Ancient Brotherhood, the word "Magic" appears across the middle and the sacred G occupies the place of light in the center.

T	U	R	N	S		1	4	2	8	5	7		M	E	M	P	E
E	H	O	O	K		16	15	1	2				Y	A	P	S	Y
M	A	G	I	C		4	3	13	14				R	I	G	O	A
P	O	I	I	O		5	10	8	11				D	I	S	I,	C
L	E	V	E	L		9	6	12	7				H	I	N	K	C

(VENUS TAROT — NUMBER 777)

At the other side a magic square appears, that has proved a "sphinx" to all who have attempted its solution thus far. It was evidently constructed by a brother of the Order, as appears in the diagonal line, but what the meaning can be no one knows. Some think it has some connection with our Temple at Memphis, while others fail to see it that way. At any rate the words are unintelligible to moderns and will remain so until some person solves the riddle. The only explanation that has survived and come down to us with it, is that it contained a secret of the Order, the key to which was thrown away by a "brother of the sacred line." It was placed in the mystic chart in order that all mystics might have a chance to study it.

We have only given a few points in this work, upon a subject that is practically infinite. We have given enough, however, to lead any mystic mind forward in a search for more light. The light will be found, too, by those who seek for it in the right spirit. We know, of course, that thousands who read this book will feel an ambition to be able to exhibit the mystic powers that they have read of. To all such we would respectfully say, that the secret source of knowledge, from whence comes the astonishing prognostications that have bewildered sages and philosophers and all classes of people, are now open to but a few.

The world had to wait two thousand years for even one to receive the. mantle and be invested with the tremendous responsibility. He who is not fit to be a student, cannot hope to aspire to be a teacher.

Again, the truth should be able to stand alone, regardless of he who utters it. You do not need a commission from on high to enable you to help in spreading the light.

Friends, we are nearly at the end of our present edition. Weigh well the proofs given here of a divine purpose, a divine plan; not the arbitrary wish or thought of one being, one soul, but *the concensus of all soul, all being.*

Consider the mathematical demonstrations exhibited in this work and in other works upon co-ordinating lines, and then ask yourselves the question:

COULD ALL THIS COME BY CHANCE?

We should emphatically say not. Men may juggle with mere words, which are at best but arbitrary representatives of ideas. We see this done in the pulpit and upon the rostrum, as well as in the press. But *figures are facts.* Figures *will not lie.* They have the habit of speaking truth in *tones of thunder.* All the arguments ever brought up against the dogmas of the church, would not have shaken her hold upon the minds of the people in an age. But the cold, sharp, unyielding and glittering blade of the sword of truth, has been wielded by the mailed hand of mathematical law, and the props of superstition are gradually but surely yielding and falling before its tremendous sweep.

The first chapter of Genesis has been smashed by the figures of geology. The story of Joshua and the Sun, has been knocked to atoms by the figures of astronomy.

The man-made Jehovah of the Bible has been driven out of his place in the heavens, by the wondrous figures of Siderial investigation. The ridiculous idea of ascending into heaven bodily, being resurrected in the flesh and going to heaven in that form, together with hundreds of other childish conceptions of the past, are gradually being wiped out by the figures belonging to philosophy, chemistry and other scientific branches.

Last, but not least, the old conception of the human soul and body existing by some act of special creation; or the grandest product of the earth, the human mind, the entity, being the growth of a few weeks; or a few months, together with the erroneous belief that " man controls his own destiny," or, in fact, is anything else but a creature of the Law, all must in turn fall, before the sublime demonstrations furnished by the FIGURES OF MYSTICISM.

Test Book Supplement.

HE first edition of the MYSTIC TEST BOOK was but fairly out when we realized that many persons could not understand what we thought such plain directions for laying a grand spread as are given on pages 56 and 57. Some could not understand "which side to sit on," or whether lines ran across or lengthways. To aid the understanding of this important subject, I have had an engraving made of a spread laid on a table, with the planets at the end of each planetary line, place of sitter and reader, sun cards and all complete. The cards are laid from the side of the delineator to the other side for each planet, beginning with Mercury and ending with Neptune, and then the last three in same way to the sun row at top. The "Life Lines run up and down the table, crossing the planetary lines.

Some persons write to me to know "which one of the

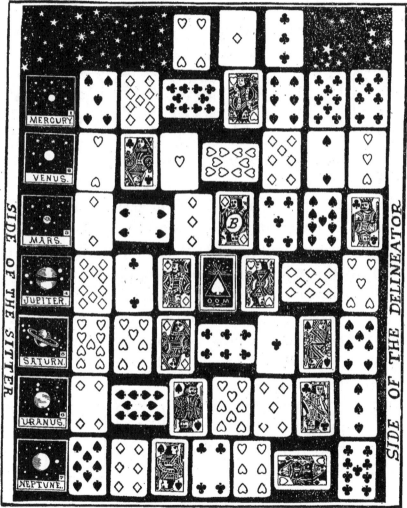

various definitions given under a card in the tables is the right one." To this question I can only say that "cast-iron rules" cannot be given in such a work. I give the various meanings as nearly as possible. The delineator must con_ sider the environments of the person and the positions of other cards in the layout, in determining which is the correct definition. Sometimes more than one of the clauses are indicated simultaneously.

The following delineation is made on the above spread and the cards reproduced by lines to make it plainer:

DELINEATION UNDER MERCURY.

The past shows an obstacle to your gaining certain knowledge which you have craved, which obstacle you have greatly overcome through your power and perseverance. You have shown much courage, and have worked steadily until, by the help of a middle-aged gentleman, who is a good friend to you, you have achieved success in gaining knowledge which largely effects your future success. A sudden disappointment will arise, in a pecuniary way, before many months; a change of employment and a journey will be necessitated thereby.

DELINEATION UNDER VENUS.

Indecision and perplexity regarding a love affair is indicated in the past; and a co-partnership or undertaking with a lady, which terminated unfavorably and caused the loss of some money to yourself. You have many friends at present, and make friends easily.   One person loves you very truly; but the ace of hearts following the ten shows that the love is kept secret and will not be revealed for some time to come. You have a friend, who is a very intelligent lady.   You will see her many times during the coming year, and you will enjoy her society very much.   You will gain much knowledge of her, which will be a great satisfaction to you, as you have an ardent love of wisdom and knowledge.   A union of hearts is indicated, and a possible marriage in the near future.

DELINEATION UNDER MARS.

A military man is shown in your past, and he has had considerable influence over you.   Quite a disappointment has been caused by the ill success of a certain man whom you intrusted with a business matter.   A change was thereby produced in your affairs, and a quarrel which is yet pending. A youngish gentleman, a lawyer, is a friend of yours, and he is a money-making man, and will prosper greatly in the future.   This man has met with a disappointment, caused by the death of a prominent man, which produced a great change in his past life.

A law suit, or some kind of a pecuniary matter, with considerable uncertainty attached, eventually results satisfactorily for your interests and labor.   A co-partnership with a gentleman in some pecuniary undertaking is shown in the future under the planet.

DELINEATION UNDER JUPITER.

A business journey is shown in the past, which changed the conditions of yourself and a friend, and resulted in a pecuniary transaction in which the friend made more money than you did. There is a secret now between two gentlemen regarding that business transaction.

In the future, the king of diamonds indicates a wealthy man whom you will obtain a co-partnership with, in which you will contribute certain knowledge which you possess. This is shown by the two of clubs. The ten of diamonds indicates great success in this enterprise, and you will make considerable money through the co-partnership.

DELINEATION UNDER SATURN.

The seven of spades shows in the past an illness of some lady. This illness interfered with a wish which you had to gain certain knowledge, and in consequence the opportunities for gaining that particular information have been unsatisfactory and monotonous. You will soon meet a lady of means and business capacity and great abilities, who will exert considerable influence over your affairs. You will grow to love her, but will meet with a rejection, or at least with a rebuff. The nine of hearts indicates a disappointment in love, and following the seven, shows a quarrel. The entire layout under Saturn indicates more or less trouble in your love affairs.

DELINEATION UNDER URANUS.

The three of spades shows an indecision regarding a journey, which is connected with some kind of work and a business transaction in which a real estate dealer, shown by the knave, bears an important part. The five of diamonds shows that an actual transaction in real estate was made, which resulted in better opportunities and more power for yourself. Another real estate dealer, older than the former a man of large experience, comes into your life soon, and your labors take on a high form of success, and you gain in wealth through the sale of property.

The four of diamonds shows much satisfaction from a pecuniary standpoint, and many deals of a successful character.

DELINEATION UNDER NEPTUNE.

The nine of clubs shows a disappointment regarding a long journey which transpired a year or two ago. This journey was to be to visit a kind hearted lady, who has traveled a great deal. The six of hearts indicates a monotonous life for a time, which ends, as shown by the four of clubs, in a short, pleasant journey just completed. The knave of spades is a traveling man, whom you will soon meet and travel with for a time. The journey will be monotonous, although pecuniary successful

The eight of spades shows a business interest at a distance, and a control of many laborers. Concentration of efforts.

A GENERAL DELINEATION.

The ruling sun card—ace of diamonds—indicates that an ardent desire you once had for riches has now departed. The three of clubs shows that a certain indecision regarding a religious opinion or doctrine has departed. The four of hearts in the sun shows that a satisfaction you once enjoyed in the love of a certain person has disappeared.

The future shows more brightness for you than in the past, but the disappointments are pretty near evenly balanced. A peculiar line of court cards, beginning under the past, in Neptune, extending upward to Jupiter, and then dropping down in the immediate future to Neptune, indicate that the majority of persons with whom you associate and do business with are connected and acquainted with each other. This condition will remain about one year longer, when there seems to be a complete change of associations, and a breaking up of old ties. One lady only will be your companion the latter part of your life.

Your birth card, the knave of diamonds, is immediately surrounded as follows, the card itself being indicated in the lay out by a button placed thereon:

The ten of hearts, under Venus, just above the Birth

Card, shows that you have a very affectionate and loving disposition. The ace of spades—the secret and mystic card —just below, indicates a mystic disposition and a love of secret, unusual knowledge. Your money affairs are usually in a state of indecision, and you do not feel wholly settled,

1 H   10 H   7 D
3 D   J D   5 C
K D   1 S   J H

POSITION OF PERSONS' BIRTH CARD.

and desire a change of business. This is indicated by the five of clubs and three of diamonds on opposite sides of your birth card. The cornering cards are not so significant, but the ace of hearts indicates a desire for love and affection and the jack of hearts indicates a true friend.

DELINEATION OF SIGNIFICATORS.

Significators. They are well distributed, falling, as they do, under all the seven planets. This indicates that your life, at present, is well balanced, and the three success cards ruling with you now are indicative of future success in your undertakings.

The four of spades indicates a satisfaction in your future labors. The eight of diamonds, a power in pecuniary affairs, and the six of clubs, a slow gaining of knowledge. The queen, ruling under Neptune, indicates a loving woman who affects your life strongly.

The good and bad in your life is well balanced, and the red and black emblems are not in long diagonal lines, as with many persons. This fact indicates that you do not hold to one line of thought, action or labor for a long period at a time.

Your life has presented a variety of effects and events, but not a great variety of human friendships and companionships.

TAROTOLOGY.

It is a matter of regret that we have been unable to get out a complete work on tarots ere this, as we find a large demand therefor. The work is under way, and we hope to have it out before the end of 1896.

In the meantime we will make a few additions to the matter already given.

QUADRATION OF TAROTS.

A number of Mystics have been considerably interested in this phase of tarotology, so we have resolved to extend the knowledge of it to all our readers. The quadration of a tarot makes changes therein which the ordinary duplex changes under the various planets, according to the diagrams on pages 222 and 223, do not make. The quadratic change seems to run through several different branches of a given series, and to unfold many new characteristics.

To perform the quadrate, take any card tarot—say, for example, No. 96, on page 218—and begin at the lower right-hand corner, place the first card on the one next above it. Then place the two cards on the third, and so on. When four are piled up, place the pile, still face up, on to the bottom card of next row, and so on until all are piled. In the case we have before us the eight of hearts is put on the ace of clubs, those on the five of diamonds, those on to the four of spades, and those on to the two of spades, and so on, ending with the ace of spades.

Now turn the cards over and deal the two top ones face

down on the table, together, not changing the order of them.
Let us say there is a Zodiac on the table, for the purpose of
this description, although not necessary for the experiment.
Say you put the first two cards in the heart quarter. Now
put the next two in the second, or club quarter; the next
two in the third, and next two in the fourth, and so on again
until all are dealt. Now gather them on to the first quarter precisely as you do in performing any quadrate.

Then lay out a new tarot by placing the top card at the
left-hand top corner, and the next to right of it, and so on,
as you would read a book. As an example, we show the
result of the first quadrate:

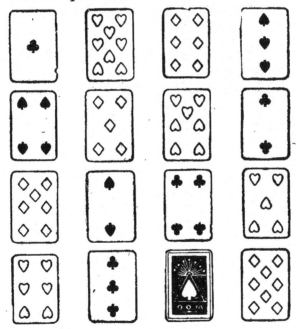

A careful examination of this tarot and the original shows
several wonderful changes, on comparison.

First, the original tarot runs two hearts with two spades

and two diamonds with two clubs on all the lines across, or what is called the duplex formation; while up and down and the **X** is quadruplex, or each line containing four suits. But the new tarot is quadruplex on all the lines except the **X**, which is duplex.

Second, the tarot is completely changed from positive to negative. If the first tarot is regarded as a Mercury tarot on the ace of spades, it has been changed into a Jupiter feminine tarot.

Furthermore, every male square emblem has changed over to a female square. No other manipulation known can so completely change a tarot in its characteristics.

An examination of the last engraving will show any one the transformation which takes place under quadration. Starting with No. 1, we have a duplex formation; that is, all four suits on all the lines except the diagonals, with one court card on each line everywhere. No. 2 is a female duplicate, quadruplex *on all the lines*. No. 3. is a male duplex tarot; that is, all the lines are in two suits, except the X. No. 4 is the fifth quadrate, again it is a full quadruplex. I have not called attention to half the changes, but the Mystic reader will notice the way the court cards change, and other things about it.

This series of tarots also has the peculiarity of the "spot values" adding thirty-four, exactly the same as the number tarots.

In No. 4 we find the conditions of suit formation restored, as in No. 2. But the tarot is changed in sex, and the position of the colors are, therefore, exactly reversed.

In many tarots the quadrate may be gathered on to other piles than the heart quarter, and there are some which can be cut and then quadrated, still forming perfect tarots, Some of our members have quadrated their individual tarots in all ways possible, and have recorded each result in a book for purposes of study.

The change taking place in the next tarot shows the usual quadruplex changes, and also changes the duplex positions of the emblems, so that such appear only in the X.

In all of this we have not taken note of the spirits of the emblems. But the same wonderful changes have manifested themselves there, as well as in the physical. Wherever the physical is displaced anywhere there is always a corresponding astral movement, which is usually even greater in influence than the physical movement.

QUADRATE OF TAROT NO. 122, PAGE 216.

MOVEMENTS UNDER QUADRATION.

The movement which takes place with any particular number under successive quadrations is peculiar.

On the succeeding page an engraving will be found, which graphically illustrates the four phases under quadration.

The same diagrams also illustrate the movements of all the emblems by one quadration.

Diagram A gives the movements which take place on one line, and B on another. In addition to this there are two movements called "vibrators," which *correspond exactly to the vibrators of the triple quadrate* which form the cross in the heavens. DiagramC shows the vibrators.

It is a curious fact that A, turned bottom up, is exactly the same as B, yet it takes both movements to cover all the tarot except the vibration squares.

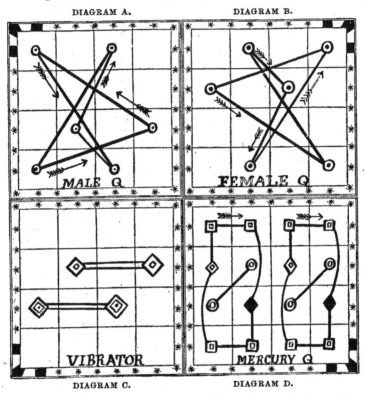

DIAGRAM A.   DIAGRAM B.

DIAGRAM C.   DIAGRAM D.

Now, if we take a tarot and quadrate it, and then "trans-form" it under Jupiter, according to diagram three, on page 222, we have a female Mercury tarot. The entire movement from the original Mercury tarot is very regular in a quadri latural motion, as illustrated in diagram D. The arrows show the direction of the movements.

By an examination of diagram D we notice that each line it composed of the emblems which, in the original, occupied the corners of quadrilaterals, and therefore we are able to formulate the general law that—

Any tarot can be quadrated to a perfect tarot when the four perpendicular and four horizontal parallelograms are perfect thirty-fours.

With card tarots this is a common characteristic, but with "*number*" birth tarots I know of but three hundred and eighty-four which have the perfection of quadratic formation. There are other series, however, which exhibit the

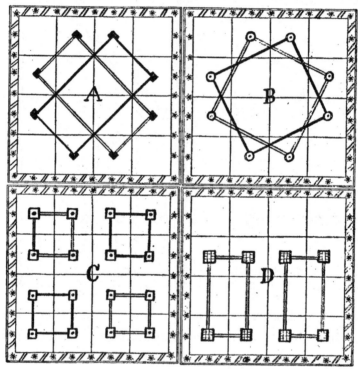

quadratic thirty-fours in other situations. This series has been called "the wonder series," but another series, which is first cousin to it, called the "cross series," is even more wonderful; so I have named the other "the quadratic series."

We will take specimens and exhibit the peculiarity mentioned, as one would scarce notice it unless attention was

particularly called to it. These quadratic tarots are called
Sun tarots in the Quadratus used in the Temple at Chicago.

BIRTH TAROTS OF THE QUADRATIC SERIES.

1	12	8	13		12	1	13	8		5	16	4	9
15	6	10	3		6	15	3	10		11	2	14	7
14	7	11	2		7	14	2	11		10	3	15	6
4	9	5	16		9	4	16	5		8	13	1	12

The marvelous number of quadratic forms, which add up
thirty-four in the above tarots, is best understood by refer-
ring to the diagrams. A, B, C and D contain ten quadratic
thirty-fours. In the next illustration, E, F, G and H con-

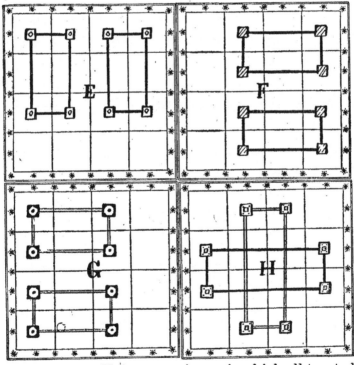

tain eight more   H, however, is a pair which all tarots have.
It is, like the quadrate of the four corners and four inner
squares, common to all tarots.

Now, to sum up all the thirty-fours in one of these numerical tarots:

Quadratics on diagrams A, B, C, D 10
Quadratics on diagrams E, F, G, H.................... 8
Corner and center quadrates, common.................
Diagonals of tarots, **X**,............................
Perpendicular lines..................................
Horizontal lines.....................................

Total........................30
Common to all tarots...............................14
Extra above the least quadratic......................16

Just equal to the number of squares in the birth tarot.

The following specimens are tarots of the wonderful "cross" series, so called because a number of them are used in the unfoldment of the magic cube into the magic cross. They are not only remarkable from their quadratic qualities, but they all have the strange peculiarity that any line can be taken off of any side and moved to the other side, or top to bottom anywhere, without injury to the tarot.

1	8	11	14		1	15	10	8		1	14	4	15
15	10	5	4		12	6	3	13		12	7	9	6
6	3	16	9		7	9	16	2		13	2	16	3
12	13	2	7		14	4	5	11		8	11	5	10

SPECIMENS OF CROSS TAROTS—MALE.

There are 384 of these tarots on record in the archives of the Magi. On page 274 we give the celebrated "Tarot Cross," from one of the Grand Temple charts. It is worthy of careful study, as it shows wonderful characteristics, which go to prove that the "Cross," as a magic emblem, belongs to the Magi.

Originating in the southern heavens, in shining stars, it belongs to the "*Religion of the Stars.*"

It is also formed from the unfolding of the geometrical "magic cube," held in such high estimation by the ancients.

The peculiar quality of "side tranposition" belonging to the cross tarots is such that we can place many tarots together in a section, from which we can take as many squares

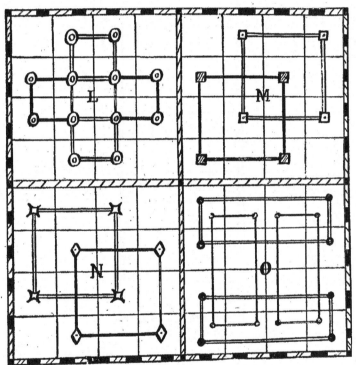

of sixteen as we please in any direction, side ways or bottom up, and half of these will be perfect tarots. In some card tarots every square is perfect.

The diagram on this page illustrates some of the quadratics not given in preceding diagrams. Now examine the cross tarots carefully, and note the wonderful quadruplex

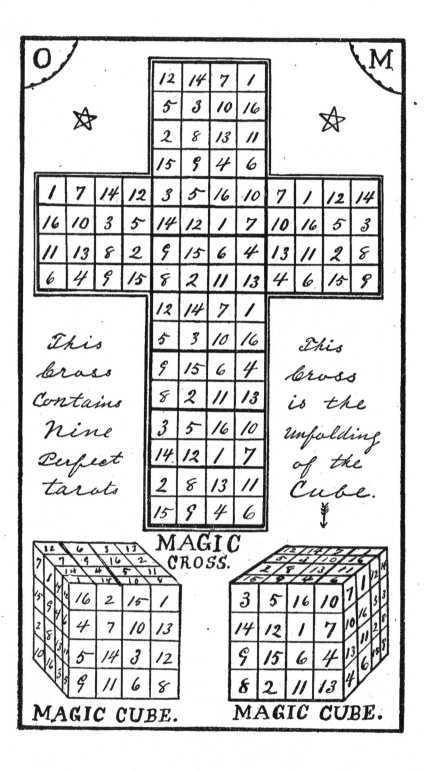

MAGIC CROSS.

This cross contains nine perfect tarots

This cross is the unfolding of the cube.

MAGIC CUBE.

MAGIC CUBE.

character of them. Remember that the common thirty-fours, or what are called "constants," number fourteen. Of "variables," as they are called, a cross tarot has as follows:

Quadrilaterals like diagram A.... 2

      "   "   "   C... 4

                      L... 4

                    M... 2

                    N.... 2

      "   O.... 4

Total variables................,...18

Total constants 14

Grand total...............32

In other words the quadratic and line thirty-fours are equal to just twice the squares of the tarot. There are still other quadratic thirty-fours not given in the above. Some tarots have few; others nearly as many as the samples exhibited. The tarot which represents a given person has the qualities of the person so represented. Some persons have high geometrical natures, others are low geometrically. This is beautifully illustrated in the combination or super-imposing of tarots of males and females. But that subject cannot be taken up in this work, but will be fully exemplified in the work which I shall soon publish. devoted exclu sively to tarotology.'

As a curiosity we herewith give a tarot with very slight quadruplex character. To the right will be found the Quad-rate of it:

An examination of No. 2 will show that the quadrate has knocked out every thirty-four in it, except the diagonals **X**, and they have survived the wreck by being composed of the two common quadrates, **H**, of diagram on page 271.

9	1	16	8		3	10	14	15
12	4	5	13		8	13	1	4
6	14	11	3		11	2	6	7
7	15	2	10		16	5	9	12

SINGLE FEMALE, NO MATE.   SAME QUADRATED.

We also find, from this illustration, that the **H** quadrilaterals of one tarot form the **X** of the next in the quadratic chain.

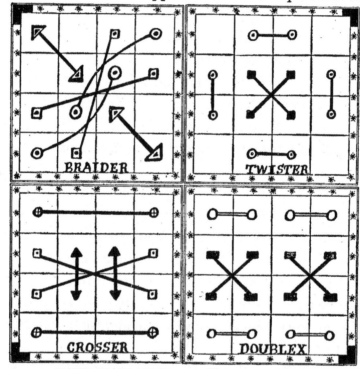

BRAIDER   TWISTER

CROSSER   DOUBLEX

GENERAL TRANSFORMATION OF TAROTS.

Some of my students have requested me to exhibit some of the general changes which can be applied to all tarots, which while changing part of the tarot, leave other parts intact. There are a large number of such changes, some of which only apply to particular kinds of tarots. In the next illustration the first three are general transformers. The lines show which numbers are to be exchanged. Number 4 is a transformer of only the XX tarots, so called because the transformation makes a double X in the middle of the tarot. No. 1 is called the "Braider;" No. 2, the "Crosser;" No. 3, the "Twister," by manipulators of the tarot blocks or emblems.

All these devices apply with even greater power to the tarots of the mystic text book.

SAMPLES OF DOUBLE X TAROTS.

1	8	15	10		1	14	12	7		1	15	12	6
4	14	5	11		6	15	9	4		7	14	9	4
13	3	12	6		11	2	8	13		10	3	8	13
16	9	2	7		16	3	5	10		16	2	5	11

The XX tarots all have the characteristics of the "Star" B formation (see page 270). Tarots of the A formation can be transformed from male to female by simply moving the two outside lines in, and the inside lines out. See same diagram for A.

CO-ORDINATING TWELVES.

There is a regular system of co-ordinations existing between the various combinations of twelves and the outer circle of the tarot. This is entered into more fully in the work of the Cabala; but I will give a few of the pointers in this work, preparatory to that more advanced. The first illustration of this series gives the house signs of the Zodiac, with the four planets occupying the "sun place," which rule the characteristics of the quarters.

Uranus, in the first quarter, signifies spirituality. Neptune signifies knowledge gained by travel; Mars, conquests by force, and Mercury short journeys by land or water.

SIGNS OF THE ZODIAC CO-ORDINATED.

The next illustration shows the months of the year co-ordinated in the same manner. The spring months coming in the heart quarter, ruled by Venus. The fall, under Jupiter, ruler of wealth, and the winter, or death months, under Saturn, the spade ruler.

The Earth, in the fall of the year, when the crops are turned to wealth, in September, October, and November, represents the diamond quarter.

In the co-ordination of the Tribes, Jupiter represents "Power" in the Club quarter; Mercury, sex love in the

Heart quarter; Mars, conquest of Arms in the Diamond quarter; Saturn representing death in the Spade quarter.

MONTHS CO-ORDINATED.

The third illustration of this series exhibits the co-ordinations of the twelve tribes of Israel in their relations to the mystic tarot. Remember that this wonderful arrangement is borne out and proved by the laws of the Cabala, which work I shall hereafter bring out.

THE TWELVE TRIBES OF ISRAEL.

The entire Jewish Cabala, in fact the entire bible, presents a mass of evidence regarding the mathematical arrangement of all the twelves, and their names fit exactly into the tarot squares. So also do the Disciples of Jesus fit the Zodiac

and the tarots.   The next illustration exhibits the arrangement of the twelve Disciples, according to the tarot and
Cabala laws.

There is a strange circumstance in connection with this
set of twelves.   Judas comes in the " house of death," and
the quarter of Saturn, the planet of death, and he was the

THE RULINGS OF THE TWELVE TRIBES.

one who betrayed the Master with a kiss.   Furthermore,
when Judas was out of the circle the other Disciples chose
another one to take his place. and this one exactly takes
the place of Judas in the Cabala of Magic, which will be
seen when that work is published.   Judas is not placed in
the house of Pisces arbitrarily, but he comes there according
to the Bible and the law of Mysticism.

There is a deep significance to all these co-ordinating twelves, which, when properly understood, opens the door to a flood of light upon Mystic Philosophy.

THE TWELVE DISCIPLES.

Venus, in the heart quarter, representing love and friendship; Terra, the Earth, power under clubs; Neptune, representing the diamond quarter, as a diamond ruler; Saturn again signifying death.

The next cut represents the twelve stones in the breast plate of the High Priest. There are just seven stones, ruled by the seven planets, and these seven stones are all mentioned in each of the lists in Genesis and Revelations. None of the others are in both lists. One list is that of the twelve "foundation stones" of the temple upon high.

The stones ruling under the seven planets will be given
here to accommodate several persons who have asked for
them. In all this series of illustrations the reader will
find which Tribes, Disciples and Stones rule in each house of
the Zodiac, by noticing the co-ordinating places on the tarot.

THE TWELVE PRECIOUS STONES.

In the mention of these twelve stones in the bible, particular stress is laid upon the arrangement of them into "rows."
This has a peculiar significance. Perhaps, before the close
of this book, I may have a place where I can present these
stones in these "rows" for our Mystic friends to study over, in
order to see what mystic quality they have in those positions.

The next engraving shows what stones rule under the

seven planets, and also the Earth. These are the recognized rulers under the ancient reckoning, but all stones can be assigned to some planet, under the law of vibration.

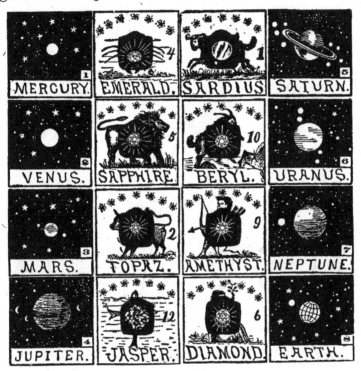

THE RULING STONES UNDER THE PLANETS.

Since the publication of the first edition of the MYSTIC TEST BOOK, Í have had a large number of letters from appreciative persons who have studied the wonderful co-ordinations set forth regarding the triangular formation of the Grand Word.

One first-class mathematician wrote: "Any person who understands the branch of mathematics applying to right-angled triangles, cannot but admit the existence of *higher intelligences* in the universe than physical men, when he observes the wonderful co-ordinating numbers of that triangle." A noted Chicago writer said: "Laying aside all mysteries, all assumption and all ordinary magic manifestations connected with that well known combination called 'playing cards,' the co-ordinations found in Prof. Richmond's demonstration of the 'Mystic Triangle,' alone is

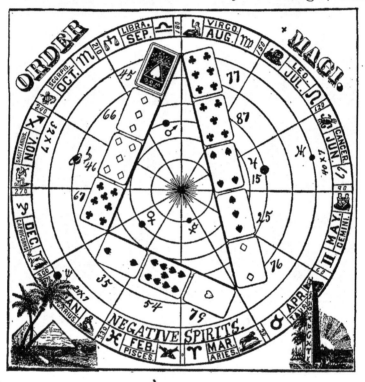

THE MYSTIC TRIANGLE.

sufficient to convince auv intelligent person of the magic —and one might almost say divine—qualities of the emblems therein." In setting forth the work, I left one very important co-ordination for my readers to discover for themselves. Some ten or twelve of them did make the discovery, and wrote and spoke to me of the same.

It is this: As wonderful as the other co-ordinations are, even the spirit values are thrown into the shade by the strange fact that the *negative* spirits also co-ordinate and form *another perfect* triangular representation of the *word.*

The diagram of negative spirits given herewith on page 284 illustrates this wonderful expression.

The negative spirits of the Base add up...........168

The negative spirits of the Perpendicular add up..224

The negative spirits of the Hypotenuse add up....280

The square of 168=28224

The square of 224=50176

The square of 280=78400

Showing a perfect right-angled triangle.

I have said nothing heretofore regarding the interweaving of the sacred 7, in this work, of the triangle. I will notice a little of it here. Out of just 24 figures representing the negative spirits, that is equal to the hours in a day, one-fourth of them are sevens. That is a much larger per cent-age than would come under a law of "chance," one-tenth being the average.

Then, again, seven times twenty-four *these same numbers* make 168, the base of the negative spirit triangle.

Seven times the Solar Constant, 32, is equal to 224, the perpendicular. The sum of the squares of 24 and 32=1600, the square root of which, 40, multiplied by 7=280, the hypotenuse of the negative triangle. This shows clearly that the 7 is not in there by chance, but for business. In my opinion, there is more divine law and inspiration illus-trated in that triangle, as a whole, than can be found in all the "sacred" books in the world, except one.

THE QUADRATIC EMBLEMATIC CROSS.

If we take a " solar book," which is one arranged according to the solar values of the emblems, and deal it onto the Zodiac from Aries around to Pisces, placing the four last on the Sun, we get an arrangement as illustrated in the next engraving. Now if we triple quadrate them from the solar test book, and then lay them on again in the same way, we will find that four of the emblems have "vibrated," or exchanged places. The ace of clubs changes with the two of hearts, while the nine of hearts exchanges with the seven of diamonds. This exchange is marked on the diagram,

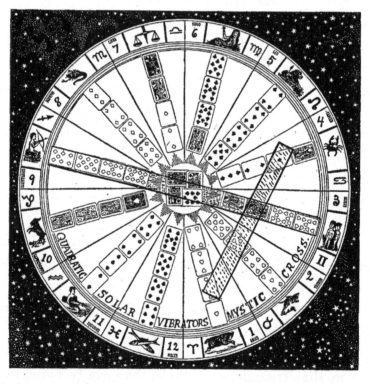

and the two vibrations form the " Shadow of the Cross," as it has been called.

On the cross, where the horizontal crosses the upright shaft, the jack of hearts is found, and he remains there, no matter how many quadrations are made, with the king of spades at the bottom.

As the jack of hearts represents the "Christ principle" in nature, this emblematic representation is interesting, from the fact that it is naturally mathematically fixed, and not arbitrary. In that respect the remarks applied to the mystic triangle will hold good here.

THE PERIHELION CROSS.

Although the layout above shown starts at Aries, at the lower Celestial Meridian, the natural Zero point of the present day, and thereby exhibits the Quadratic Cross lying across the Zodiac, it is far more in accordance with esoteric practice to begin the deal of the layout in Cancer.

First, the year begins there, the Earth starting in on its long journey from Cancer. Second, it is the perihelion of the Earth. Third, it is a point in the heavens which seems to have been universally selected by mankind for the birth of Saviors—that is, a point near the Apsides. In the case of Jesus, the date comes within less than four degrees of that line.

The layout which produces the Cross from the perihelion deal is shown in the next engraving, and, to make the Cross more striking, the rest of the cards are omitted, and the ones only put in which are covered by the Cross.

This arrangement seems to be even more remarkable than the other, for the foot of the Cross sets in Pisces, which *rules the feet*, but it is also the "house of death," in Mystic symbolism.

The top of the cross is in Virgo. It is a significant fact that the representative of Christ on the Cross comes in the House of the Virgin. He is "born" there and remains there. Another thing is worth noticing, too; that is, that, although there are two success cards on the cross, they are outweighed by the two nines and two sevens, indicating

QUADRATIC SOLAR VIBRATOR CROSS FROM PERIHELION LAYOUT.

disappointment and trouble. I was showing this Cross to a Mystic friend a while ago, when he exclaimed: "Oh! see the nail holes!" He pointed to the ace of clubs on the left and the two of hearts on the right hand. Everything goes to show that the Christ, or Divine principle, is one of those fixed things, like the mystic word triangle, which is bound to come out in the mystic emblems. Any unprejudiced person can see with half an eye that the little book, which is a "Cross" to carry before the world, has within itself the perfection of divine symbolism. As the author of the "Pappus Planetarium" enthusiastically exclaimed once to me: "That little book has got the whole history of the world in it, if we knew how to read it." I think he was pretty near right. Every time I attempt to write about it I am overwhelmed with new and more wonderful developments.

Oh, but it is a heavy cross to carry, there is no mistake about that

GENERAL LAWS GOVERNING MYSTIC EMBLEMS.

Every division of time, used by men, has its particular ruling card.

Thus, in addition to year cards and day cards, there are hour cards, minute cards, and even second cards, ruling in various orders, co-ordinating with the time elements. All these cards play an important part in all mystic work with the test book, but the finer divisions are naturally used the most. One quality of the hour cards is to fix the culminating effect of several persons in a certain class. The quality of the minute card is to fix the time element to small arc, and as this card bears a perfectly ascertainable ratio to solar, and through that to secular time; the time can always be corrected thereby. The second card of time is also a definite quality, but is momentary in effect, with a lap of two and one-half seconds on each side. By this, I mean that, suppose a certain card rules at 44 seconds culmination. The same card rules co-ordinatily, but with less power, during 42, 43, 45 and 46 seconds. This is called the five second variation.

The normal minute and second cards always bear a definite ratio to the movement of the earth, or what is the same thing, "time." But the minute and second cards of persons bear a perfect ratio to the card ruling on the day of birth, with the effect of the normal card.

Day cards and birth cards are the same thing, as the day card of to-day is the birth card of any child born to-day.

THE MINUTE CARD OF TIME.

The next engraving illustrates those important rulers, the minute cards, displayed in a miscellaneous manner, and yet

exactly under the law. You can shuffle the emblems and spread them as many times as you please, and each one will occupy a place on the table according to exact law.

But these in the illustration are normal minute cards and do not appertain to any persons' magnetism.

If you turn over the emblems shown in the cut, so that they face the Alter Cloth, they will show what planets and houses they rule under.

THE LAW OF POSITION

Cards next to the cloth rule under the Earth or Jupiter. Cards on the top of piles rule under Mercury or Saturn. Cards next to the top are under Venus or Uranus.

Cards third from the top rule under Mars or Neptune. Cards on the Sun rule under a planet and the Sun and are called "Solar Emblems."

In the cut the ten of diamonds rules under Jupiter in Leo. The King of Spades Under Earth and Sun.

The ten of hearts rules under Venus in Pisces. The nine of hearts is under Saturn in Taurus.

The King of Spades is the Solar Zero Time Card, as he is in the Solar book.

The rule published in the former edition of this book, was found to be useless for the present Century; so we only publish the old version of it. It is only used in predictions.

Rule for finding the Minute Card of Time.

Take the hour of Solar time.

Multiply it by two.

Add the Minutes of Solar time.

Multiply by the Number Seven.

The product is the "Time Product."

Take the day card of the day, annex 12 to its solar value
and add the number so produced to the "time product."

Divide the sum by 13, and divide the quotient so arising
by 4. Add 1 to the last remainder.

The remainder from the first division is the "spot value."
That from the second, the "suit number."

Remember that suit numbers run H=1, C=2, D=3, S=4.
In case there is no remainder at the first division, it indicates a king, and you do not add 1 to the second remainder,

THE RULING EMBLEM OF THE HOUR.

Each *Solar Hour* has its ruling emblem, from the time the
Earth starts on its annual tour at midnight, December 31st,
to the end of the astronomical year. These emblems are
"normal" rulers, by virtue of the polarity of the Earth, so
that each year has the same set clear through, except upon
Leap Years there is a slight variation on the given days.
The next engraving exhibits the months, with the "month
day" immediately under each month. The table is for
normal years, On Leap year add one day after Feb. 29.

The hours start at midnight; so, after noon we must add
twelve hours to the clock time to get the hour of the day.
Also, if you desire to do fine work you must make the nec-
cessary correction in time, if your timepiece is set on standard time instead of solar. In no place is the variation
intended to be over 30 minutes, so a rough estimate can be
made without going into fine details in most places. If
your longitude is west of your standard meridian, your
standard time is too fast, and *vice versa*. The correction is
about one minute for each sixteen miles variation. In

degrees the correction is four minutes to each degree, as a given point on the earth moves fifteen degrees per hour.

NORMAL MONTH DAYS.

The next engraving exhibits the normal rulers as if thrown carelessly upon the Zodiac, but each emblem occupies a place fixed by absolute magnetic law. No. 1, in each house, is the card under all the others. No. 2 is next, and so on to top one. The sun counts as 0 in the scheme of the Zodiac.

RULE FOR FINDING THE HOUR RULER.

Take the "month day," the day of the month, the hour in the day—add them together. Divide the sum by the weeks in a year, and mark the *remainder* X. Drop the quotient. Add the months in a year to X. Add the days in a week. Divide the sum by four. Add the value X to the *quotient*. Divide the sum by five.

The quotient shows the number of the house, and the remainder the place in the house of the ruling hour card.

NOTE.—As a usual thing, the card next above rules the next hour, and so on—a fact which may be helpful to students.

THE HOUR CARDS IN THE LAYOUTS.

In the fifty-two layouts, or spreads, given in this book, several of our Mystics have made the discovery that after

NORMAL RULERS OF THE HOURS.

any given card, taking it all through the fifty-two normal spreads, comes an hour ruler just twenty-four times. For instance, the ace of spades rules twenty-four times to the right of the eight of hearts, the jack of diamonds twenty-four times at the right—counting downward when at the end of the line—of the ace of spades. So, strange to say, these hour rulers, or "Earth Cards," never vary from twenty-four in each case, and all rule in fours into each other. This is a thing no other set of emblems do in those layouts; and it clearly exhibits the even passage of the Earth through the four quarters, or quadratures—a thing no other planet does on co-ordinating time, corresponding to the Test Book. For instance, the next, or second card to the right from any given emblem, rules ten times; the next, eight, and the next, three. There are just as many cards ruling after any card as there are planets—no more and no less—aside from the Earth Card before mentioned.

But all the planet cards form under each planet a *continuous chain of the whole test book,* instead of forming chains of four, as the hour cards do.

EIGHT CARDS WHICH RULE AFTER ACE OF SPADES.

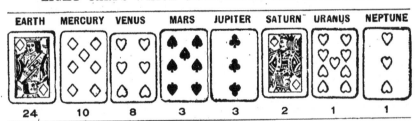

Under each emblem is the number of times it rules under that planet.

RULERS AFTER THE EIGHT OF HEARTS.

Names of planets and numbers are just the same all the way through, remember.

RULERS AFTER QUEEN OF HEARTS.

It would require fifty-two rows like the above to give all the rulers, and would require too much space, yet these rulers are very interesting, because they are the normal rulers, which are different entirely from the solar rulers found from the solar quadrate. Thus, a person born under the ace of spades would have as solar rulers under Mercury, 7 of hearts; Venus, 7 of diamonds; Mars, 5 of spades; Jupiter, jack of hearts; Saturn, 9 of clubs; Uranus, 9 of spades; Neptune, 2 of hearts, while his normal rulers would be as above given under ace of spades. There seems, in most cases heretofore examined by us, a kind of co-ordination between the solars and normals. Thus there are two sevens in each case, and a nine to balance one of the nines in the solar. The co-ordination seems to be more on the "general indications" than on same cards. When it is more fully known what the significations are of these rulers we shall publish the full table.

It has also been discovered that rulers at *all distances* from a given card are as uniform as the primary rulers. Thus, there are an exact number of cards ruling seven places to the right or left of any given card. This is also interesting, and the facts discovered by means of these tables have thrown a flood of light upon the movements of the emblems, and has led to the discovery of the new differential calculus in use in our temples.

The next illustration is designed to show the natural Zodiac emblems thrown on the circle, each in its own house, and is another way of showing the wonderful manner in

NATURAL CIRCLE OF ZODIAC CARDS.

which the Test Book fits the Zodiac. This arrangement is regardless of the planets, as the presence of a planet in any house would change the suits in their relations to each other.

THE MYSTIC STORY OF ATLANTIS.

There is a very pretty and interesting story in connection with the Test Book, which, when properly told and illustrated, attracts interest to our work and, at the same time, affords recreation. The writer has related it many times, to the amusement of his friends. Although there is nothing "occult" about it, except the knowledge of how to do it, it is none the less mysterious to the uninitiated.

You begin to sort out all the twelve picture cards, and, as you do so, start to tell the story as follows:

"Once on a time—many, many ages ago—there was an island in the Atlantic Ocean called 'Atlantis.' It was a very large island, with mountains and plains, lakes and rivers, upon it, and it was cultivated by a busy population.

"The island was divided into four quarters by large rivers which arose in the highest portion, among the mountains and from their common sources, and flowed to the ocean in four different directions. The four parts of the island were kingdoms, and four kings thus governed the entire island.

"At the great city, which was builded at the junction, or starting point of these rivers, the capitol of all the kingdoms was located, where the four Kings and their Courtiers and their Queens and wise men used to meet to pass laws and hold council together.

One chamber was set apart expressly for the sittings of the High Council, which was held once each month. In this chamber the four kings used to sit on the highest row of seats, thus:

[Place the four kings in a row on the table, in any order they may happen to come in.] .

"Upon the next seat below the kings, the queens were seated, ready to take part in the deliberations, if called upon.

[While saying this, arrange the queens in your hand carelessly in such a way that the two center ones shall be of the same suit and in the same order as the two kings at the left end of the row. Then lay them down, as if carelessly, in such a manner that the right-hand queen is the same suit as the king above her, and the two "arranged ones" in the middle, thus:]

" On the lowest seat the Prime Ministers of the four courts were seated.

[At these words, you lay the four knaves in the same order as to suit as the kings are laid.]

"After the Council was over, the various members composing it would change their positions and converse upon the subjects considered.

[As you say these words, exchange the right-hand queen with the left. Move the two left-hand knaves, in same order, and exchange them with the right-hand ones. Then exchange any king, queen or knave with any other card of *same suit*, as much as you please, while keeping up a suitable story. We will suppose now that the cards are as follows, as shown on next page.

[The changes made having produced this (although there are thousands of ways which give an almost endless variety to it). Now gather

the emblems exactly as directed for tarot quadration on page 264.
Then have any number of persons cut them, at the same time saying:]

"When the Council finally adjourned they all used to go
out to the great banqueting hall, and would become mixed
together like this:

[Pick up the cards and begin to deal them one at a time around the
four quarters of the table, saying:]

"After the banquet they all retired to the respective quarters of the palace, each king with his own queen and prime
minister."

[If all this has been done correctly, sure enough, on turning them
over, they are found to have divided in just that manner.]

THE CROSS OF OM.

I have said, heretofore, that the "Cross" belongs to

mysticism, and the universal Religion of the Stars, as proven by the numerous examples we have in tarots, stars, etc. In the Grand Temple at Chicago, we have a cross on a large chart, called the "Cross of OM," which I have reproduced for the benefit of our readers at a distance.

This Cross possesses certain mathematical qualities which make it a co-ordination nearly as remarkable as the mystic triangle or the sextuple star.

First. It contains exactly the Test Book, 52 emblems complete. It is perfect in geometrical form. It has 12 rows of emblems in the upright stem, equal to the months in a year. Each row has 3 emblems typical of the 3 houses in the quarter, or months in each season of the year.

The first 3 rows at the bottom form an emblem tarot; spot values 15, solar values 54, suit values 39, or 3 tarots in one.

The next 9 emblems above constitute a perfect tarot; spots 18, suits 78, solar values 96.

The next 9 cards are all court cards, and they form a perfect tarot, with spots 36, suits 39, solar values 75. Strange to say, the spirit values of this tarot make a perfect tarot on all the lines except one diagonal. 7 lines=127, the eighth being imperfect by exactly the amount of the "spirit double," 89. The 9 emblems at the top make a perfect tarot with spots 15, suits 78, solar values 93. We thus have in the stem of the cross 4 tarots, each containing 3, making 12, equal to the houses of the Zodiac.

The arms of the Cross are strangely occult in composition. They are remarkable examples of the exhibition of *sevens*, these mystic numbers representing the planets. The spot values of each arm are 8 sevens in value. The spot value of each section is just 4 sevens. Each section has a suit

TEST BOOK CROSS OF OM.

value of just 78, the well known tarot value seen in the

upright. Each half section of each arm has a solar value of 106.

There are just 7 spades and 7 hearts in both arms of the cross. These emblems can also be placed in such a position that the spots not only add 4 sevens across, but also perpendicularly the same, thus

10	1	4	13
6	8	12	2
2	9	7	10
10	10	5	3

How remarkable it is, that after four complete 3 x 3 tarots have been taken from the Test Book the cards remaining should have so many mystic properties based upon the deific number seven.

The card representing the Christ comes in the center in his old place *on all the Crosses*. Above His head is the "Magi Card" and with Him the 3 Marys. The 12 Court Cards emblematic of the 12 Signs of the Zodiac, have *another face card with them* in this cross, making 13, which emblematizes the whole 13 points on our Altar. The whole 13 forming a beautiful "Court Diamond" in the center of the cross. Taken as a whole, what could be made beautiful, both mathematically and geometrically, both mystically and emblematically than the *Cross of our Order?*

Jesus of Nazareth *did not bear this cross*. He bore the "cross of healing," a cross which thousands upon thousands are bearing to-day. Just as no person who has not attempted to bear the Cross of OM can tell how heavy it is, no person can realize the weight of the cross of mystic healing, except he has bourn it.   Jesus bore that cross until it ended in a cross of wood.

In our day, the "cross of healing" ends in the cross of law and public reprobation, upon which many are crucified. The writer bears the Cross of OM, and has most fully realized during the past seven years, how heavy it is.   He could also take up the other, but two crosses are rather cumbersome for one person to bear.

ASTRO-PHRENOLOGICAL STUDY.

The publication of the Chart in the first edition of this book has awakened an interest in the subject, so that several readers have requested more light thereon.   A full exposi-

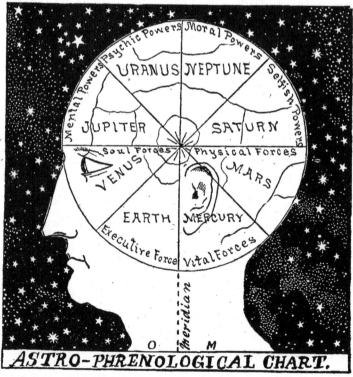

ASTRO-PHRENOLOGICAL CHART.

tion of the science of head measuring and character reading

by this process, is out of place in this work on mystic emblems; but I will give here an engraving and the principal characteristics of the divisions, as they will appear in the work to be issued later.

It may throw a little more light on the subject and lead to a further understanding of it.

LEADING CHARACTERISTICS.

UNDER MERCURY.
Amativeness.
Vitativeness.
Quick Temper.
Reproductiveness.

UNDER VENUS.
Language.
Harmony.
Perception.
Calculation.

UNDER EARTH.
Bibativeness.
Ailimentiveness.
Executiveness.
Materiality.

UNDER MARS.
Combativeness.
Conjugality.
Destructiveness.
Parental Instinct.

UNDER JUPITER.
Acquisitiveness.
Individuality.
Causality.
Locality.

UNDER SATURN.
Secretiveness.
Selfishness.
Inhabitiveness.
Continuity.

UNDER URANUS.
Sublimity.
Ideality.
Veneration.
Benevolence.

UNDER NEPTUNE.
Conscienciousness.
Approbativeness.
Firmness.
Self Esteem.

FURTHER EXPLANATION OF THE CHART.

It must be remembered that the divisions of the head are not distinct, by any means. The various dividing lines are only intended to show where the general characteristics approximately meet each other.

For instance, take "acquisitiveness," which we put under Jupiter in the table of characteristics. The quality or organ of acquisitiveness is located really at the junction of all the planetary sections, just above the ear, and extending across on an axis, coinciding with all the planets. But the characteristic named, *does* take its power from the combined effect of all the planets. Jupiter gives it direct. Venus gives us desire for wealth for our loved ones, and to attract friendship and love. Saturn, through caution, fear and selfishness, causes acquisitiveness in man. The reader will readily see how all the others center likewise.

RULINGS OF THE ZODIAC.

Although this book does not profess to be a work upon astrology, and is not, I have been requested by a number of our members to put the "Rulings of the Zodiac" in it. I have been saving these rulings for some time, expecting to put them in my work on Heliocentric Astrology, with full explanations and directions for casting horoscopes; but the publication in this work need not interfere with the project, so I may as well give the subscribers of the MYSTIC TEST BOOK the advantage of possessing them in advance of the publication of the other work. The reader will notice that there are two departments—Character and Occupation.

The small space immediately under the sign at the left of each ruling is for the purpose of entering the owners' "per centage" of standing in each house, should he ever become possessed of it. If he does not, the space does no harm.

No. 1.	MERCURY AND VENUS PREDOMINATING.
ARIES	House of the male forces or positive magnetic vibrations. Scientific thought. Head-strong. Wilfulness. Quick temper. Quick to forgive. Excitability. Feverish haste. Strong electric organization. Worry regarding immediate future. Love of lively music. Love of motion. Admiration of fine machinery. General instead of special love for opposite sex.
No. 2.	VENUS AND NEPTUNE PREDOMINATING.
TAURUS	House of the female or negative magnetic vibrations. Love of quiet and repose. Dislike of loud, boisterous persons. Tendency to worship or religion. Expectation. Anticipation. Faith and trust. Intuition. Veneration. Expression by signs instead of words. Love of harmony. Control of features to disguise true sentiments. Strong friendship. Purity. Personal adornment. Cleanliness.
No. 3. 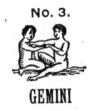 GEMINI	VENUS AND URANUS PREDOMINATING. House of parental love and harmony. Love of and care of offspring. Love of the young in general. Kindness to young animals. Incontinuity. Distrustfulness of adult persons. Restlessness under restraint. Anxiety, or a state of dissatisfaction. Restlessness. Active brain and hands. Love of knowledge.
No. 4. 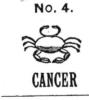 CANCER	VENUS AND SATURN PREDOMINATING. House of human nature. Love of home and family. Strong love of possession. Inclination to selfishness. Admiration of own belongings. Dislike of dictation. Kindness to own family. Love of animal pets. Susceptibility to magnetic influences. Love of table talk and a natural love of mild scandal.

No. 5. **LEO**	**MERCURY AND NEPTUNE PREDOMINATING.** House of the heart and emotions. Vital forces strong. Clinging to life. Tenacity. Vitativeness. Caution and care of self. Slyness, caused by lack of confidence in other people. Disposition for peace, unless driven too far. Can be led, but not driven. Act from the heart instead of the head. Conscientiousness. Disposition to experiment in business matters.
No. 6. **VIRGO**	**MERCURY AND URANUS PREDOMINATING.** House of the material life forces. Friendship and sociability. Love of home comforts, especially of the table. Hospitality. Alimentiveness. Dislike of low and vile persons. Sympathy with those who are persecuted. Great rallying powers. Love of bright colors. Judge of colors. Selfishness of materialistic part of organization. Personal purity and honorable conduct.
No. 7. **LIBRA**	**MARS AND JUPITER PREDOMINATING.** House of justice and trade. Disposition to fairness. Exact justice. System, method, arrangement. Bargaining and adjusting prices. Good sense of value. Suavity and politeness for sake of custom. Motives controlled by policy. Trade instinct. Practical mathematical knowledge only. Firmness combined with sagacity.
No. 8. **SCORPIO**	**MERCURY AND SATURN PREDOMINATING.** House of generation. Amativeness or strong sexual instinct. Love of physical beauty in opposite sex. Connubial love. Love of own offspring, but not of other peoples' children. Attraction towards new acquaintances of opposite sex. Exacting and impulsive. Inclined to jealousy. Strong vitality.

Life and Character Rulings of Zodiac.

NO. 9.  **SAGITTARIUS**	MERCURY AND MARS PREDOMINATING. House of energy and foresight. Prophecy based upon calculation. Activity of mind. Zealous sanguinity. Sudden impulses. Quick conclusions, sometimes incorrect. Desire to make money rapidly. To strike while the iron is hot. Demonstrative nature. Activity of body. Quick to resent fancied or real injury. Love of stories of adventure and war. Purity of love. Constancy to one person.
NO. 10.  **CAPRICORNUS**	JUPITER AND URANUS PREDOMINATING. House of executive ability and undertakings. Command of men and things. Natural leadership. Conduct of great enterprises. Money making ability. Positive nature. Quick to act in a business crisis. Determination. Impulse. Wish to always be at the head. Pride of station and wealth. Despise small things. Spiritual nature advanced and high, but kept down by material environments. Organizers.
NO. 11.  **AQUARIUS**	JUPITER AND NEPTUNE PREDOMINATING. House of water shipping and transportation. Mercantile instinct. Public good. Love of roving. Deal with many people. Wish to travel. To see the world. Active temperament. Love of water and rain storms. Bibativeness. Love of public demonstrations, brass band music, parade show and uniforms. Noise and excitement. City life. Strong intuitiveness but poor reasoners from cause to effect. Admiration of the vast and grand.
NO. 12. **PISCES**	VENUS AND JUPITER PREDOMINATING. House of Science and philosophy. Research. Acquisition of knowledge. Love of astronomy, geology and kindred sciences. Love of proven abstract and exact science instead of theories. Mathematical exactness. Care in the expenditure of money, to obtain full value therefor. Honor and uprightness. Lack of self-confidence. Fidelity to trusts. Thrift and forethought. Logical and argumentative nature.

Department of Trades and Occupations.

No. 1.  **ARIES**	MERCURY AND VENUS PREDOMINATING. Trades and professions requiring quickness of the hand and mind combined with judgment and intuition. Telegraphy. Reporting. Stenographic Work. Rapid Drawing, Sketching or Painting. String Band Playing. Teaching of Dancing. Acting. Type-setting. Writing of light literature, if any. A Male House, so the trades are mostly those followed by males as a rule.
No. 2. **TAURUS**	VENUS AND JUPITER PREDOMINATING. Trades and Professions requiring light touch, quick eyes, combined with skill and power to execute. Portrait and Landscape Painting. Drawing and Sketching where time is unlimited. Engraving in light work. Artistic Millinery, Dressmaking and Draping. Light Gardening. Artificial Flower Making. Photographing and Photo Engraving. Elocution under some circumstances. A Female House, with trades followed as a rule by females.
No. 3. 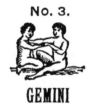 **GEMINI**	VENUS AND URANUS PREDOMINATING. Employments requiring Love of Nature and the Young, combined with Calmness and Judgment. School Teaching. Government of Children. Care of Young Children and Young Animals generally. Light Gardening. Writing of light Juvenile Literature. Poetical and Blank Verse Writing. Embroidering in Colors. Fancy Work of various kinds. Male and Female House. Avocations followed by both sexes.
No. 4. 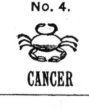 **CANCER**	VENUS AND MARS PREDOMINATING. Employments requiring Patient Labor and Domestic Love, combined with Strength to bear. Housekee ing and General Management of the family and home. Domestic Labor both outside the house and in. Sewing. Cooking. Baking. Laundry, Hotel or Restaurant Management. Boarding or Rooming. Female House. Employment mostly followed by females.

Rulings in Trades and Occupations.

NO. 5.

LEO

VENUS AND MERCURY PREDOMINATING.
Employments requiring Inspiration and Emotion, with high Magnetic Force and Power of Expression. Emotional Novel Writing. Preaching or Lecturing. Inspirational Lecturing. Some females ruling high in this, although a male house. Magnetic Healing. Mind Healing. Some kinds of Law Practice before Juries.

Male House with employments mostly of a male character.

NO. 6.

VIRGO

JUPITER AND NEPTUNE PREDOMINATING.
Employments requiring Calm, Cold Judgment without emotion and little care for others. Love of Money. Dealing in Produce, Meats and Provisions. Restaurant Keeping. Painting and Printing on a large scale. Dyeing, or any avocation requiring Judgment in Colors. Methodical Business of many kinds.

Male and Female House combined.

NO. 7.

LIBRA

JUPITER AND MARS PREDOMINATING.
Business requiring Financial Ability combined with Judgment and Will Power. Practice of Medicine as a Specialist. Manufacturing many lines of goods, or Wholesale Dealing. Retail Merchandizing. Buying and Selling generally. Trading in Lands, Horses or Stocks. Brokerage and Commission Business generally.

Male and Female House combined.

NO. 8.

SCORPIO

MARS AND URANUS PREDOMINATING.
Occupations requiring Strength and Power to bear hardship, with slight aspirations for knowledge or spiritual growth. Heavy Farming. Stock Raising. Common Labor of many kinds. Jobbing and Building Trades. Mechanical Labor. Severe Domestic Labor. Iron Working. Coal Mining. Wood Working etc.

Male House. Nearly neutral, however.

No. 9.

SAGITTARIUS

JUPITER AND URANUS PREDOMINATING.
Business requiring strong, unflinching Judgment, great Executive Ability and Management with stern Selfishness and Resolution to Succeed. Banking. Loaning. Renting. Insurance. Real Estate Dealing. Publishing. Editing. Heavy, Practical Literature. Legal Practice. Surgery. Dentistry and general Medical Practice.

Male House, with male avocations predominating.

No. 10.

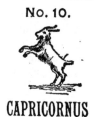

CAPRICORNUS

JUPITER AND NEPTUNE PREDOMINATING.
Undertakings requiring Ability to Organize and Control large Institutions, Governing Ability and Lavish Expenditure of Money to make money. Large Manufacturing and Jobbing of Merchandise. Superintending of Railroads, large Lines of Transportation or Express Companies. Great Organizers of Stock Companies, etc. Females often rank high in this house but cannot exercise their abilities therein.

Male and Female House combined.

No. 11.

AQUARIUS

MARS AND NEPTUNE PREDOMINATING.
Occupations requiring hardihood and strength with a Love of Out-Door Life and Water, or Dampness. Shipping or Sailing. Expressing. Milling. Mining. Engineering. Surveying. Fishing and many kindred employments. When females are high in this house they dislike indoor employments and love to travel.

Male House with male employments.

No. 12.

PISCES

MERCURY AND URANUS PREDOMINATING.
Occupations or Professions requiring quickness of Intelligence and Power to Grasp Situations, combined with Dignity and Power to Make Most of one's Personality. Office Holding or Political Power. Some Branches of Law. Managers of Offices. Many Trades and Avocations come under this. Some females are strong in this without opportunity to exercise their ability.

Male and Female House combined.

The student is cautioned against the prevailing notion, which people are prone to indulge, that these definitions are cast-iron in their rigidity. Nothing whatever, based upon the magnetism of any one body in the solar system, can be fixed absolutely.

All the Life and Character Rulings and the Rulings of

TEST BOOK "CROSS OF LOVE." *SPRING.*

Trades and Occupations are dependent upon the polarity of the Earth in its relation to the Sun. That is a definite relation enough, as far as the two bodies—the Earth and Sun—are concerned. But the other great magnets in the system, seven in number, are all the time forming different combinations relative to each other and their aspect to the earth, which fact must always be taken into consideration.

For instance, supposing a lady was born in Scorpio. Primarily, that polarity would indicate that she would be fitted for sever e domestic labor. But the effect of Saturn, in strong aspect at her birth, may give her a physical consti- tution unfitted for the strain of such labor. She would have the "disposition to make things move," in her domestic affairs, without the necessary health to back it.

TEST BOOK "CROSS OF KNOWLEDGE." *SUMMER.*

The writer was born in Virgo, but the earth had just gone out of Leo, and the planets were in such a peculiar aspect to those two houses that the effect was split, and his rulings partake of the nature of Leo fully more than of

Virgo. Many persons do not seem to understand the difference between being born *in* a sign or *under* a sign. The sign, or "house," you are born *in* is the one where the earth is at birth. The sign you are born *under* is the one where the sun is. One's rulings often partake largely of those of the sign where the sun is, which is, of course, the opposition sign from the Earth at birth.

TEST BOOK "CROSS OF WEALTH." *AUTUMN.*

The reason why the Mystic Emblems are used by us so much is because they are ths exponents of the effects of all kinds, including the earth, sun and planets and their magnetic forces. Just as a logarithm is the exponent of a given power, so the emblem is the exponent of a given effect. No matter what number is produced, let it be ever so large or ever so small, it represents the solar value of one emblem and the spirit of some emblem. Take the number 319,372 for instance: This number completely represents the Spirit of the Mystic Test Book, its spirit root being 44.

TEST BOOK "CROSS OF LABOR AND DEATH." *WINTER.*

But it represents the exponent emblem of the book, the Magi Card, Ace of spades, in three ways. It is the solar value, the spirit value and the astral value of that emblem.

The astral root of the Magi Card is 55. which is found by dividing by 7 instead of 9. The same number seldom represents all the three phases of one emblem, yet each card has many such numbers.

Pyramid Tarotology
Test Book Supplement of 1919

As the publication of all the knowledge in the possession of the Grand Temple, regarding this subject, would cost tens of thousands of dollars, I have concluded to give a brief outline of the emblem branch only; together with illustration of the altar cloth used in the work and a few sample tarots of the thousands in our records.

The Pentads, or Pyramid tarots, are the most used in magic; from the fact that they fit the zodiac in so many ways. Chart one shows this on the altar cloth. Each house having two squares; the positive being next to the sun, the negative outside. Except those which are equidistant from the sun, in which case, the first square in right ascension is positive.

Previous to the present Jurisdiction, 1844 on, mathematicians knew nothing about the Geometry of Tarots. To them all tarots looked alike; as the mathematical tarots do to this day. But the grand discovery of the "soul of the tarots" differentiated them into Generic Classes, families and branches. To the ancients, a beautiful, nicely balanced "soul tarot," looked much the same as a veritable "Straw stack." Yet one is highly evolved, while the other is low in evolution.

They correspond to humanity in many ways. They have family ties, sisters, mothers, cousins, aunts and offspring; even to the fifth generation. The traits of the

RELIGION

OF THE

STARS,

Grand Temple

of the

Order of the Magi,

Chicago.

24	6	13	2	20
17	15	1	23	9
5	22	7	10	21
8	4	25	16	12
11	18	19	14	3

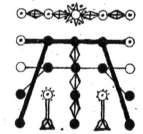

24	6	13	2	20
17	15	1	28	9
5	18	7	14	21
8	4	25	16	12
11	22	19	10	3

different kinds of tarots are entirely different. They also require different treatment, and possess different dispositions; just as human beings do. Not only that, but they differentiate in the same manner that chemical atoms and molecules do. Some families of tarots are very prolific, such as the Normal and Primo. Others are so choice and highly evolved, that only a dozen exists in the entire universe.

The Primo family has 795,680 members; only reckoning near relatives.

The Normal family has over 800,000 members; while the Marvel group is known to have sixty sub classes, with 850,000 members and more being discovered every year.

These are all mathematical tarots, made from the numbers 1 to 25 and no two alike.

All together there are only about three million figure tarots. But those made from the Mystic emblems, number into billions, and then some. Their number are like the sands of the sea shore.

When an inspired tarot is pulled out of the Infinite, by a well balanced battery of mystic souls, there is absolutely no limit to the possibilities.

The samples below the Cloth, on the Chart, show the work of two such classes of twelve members each. They were as far apart as the poles in their emblem characteristics, yet came within an Ace of being alike, mathematically. They are called the "Altars of OM."

The full use of this Cloth and its emblematic signification, can only be understood and appreciated by members of the Grand Temple, above third degree in rank.

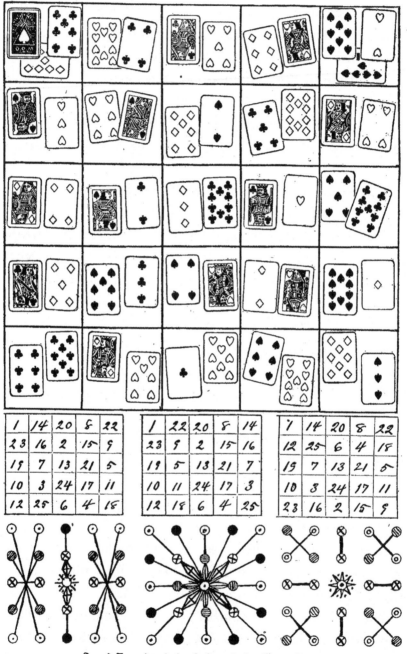

Grand Temple of the Order of the Magi, Chicago.

CHART TWO; gives an illustration of an inspired emblem lay-out; with the cards turned face up. The mathematical value of the cards are entirely different from the solar values given elsewhere in this book.

TAROTOLOGICAL VALUES.

Aces to Fives and also Tens = their spot value.

Sixes, equal their quarter value.

Seven of Hearts and all the Eights = five times their Quarter Value

The other Sevens and Nines all equal Zero.

Jacks equal five. Queens equal fifteen. Kings equal twenty.

Solar values can be used, in making Pyramid Tarots, in the same manner as shown in Chapters IX and X.

The Astrological reading of a tarot lay-out, is even more accurate and minute than the Solar Quadrate Method; but the Method cannot be given in this work. The same emblem significations are used in reading tarots as those given in the body of this work; with the added advantage of knowing what house and polarity a card is ruling in.

HOW THE SOUL OF A TAROT IS FOUND.

There are twelve pairs of mates in a Pentagonal Tarot, each pair consisting of extreme numbers which add 26. The mates are joined by a straight line in the geometric diagram.

If two pair of mates LAP on each other, the entire line is doubled by convolutions; as seen in diagrams. If one pair is entirely ON the line of another, only the ON is doubled. If the Sun is ON, the line is doubled. The 13

represents the Sun and has no mate. It is marked as a
sun, on the diagram. Where colors are used, in recording
the diagram, the characteristics of the tarot can be differentiated by the colors. But in plain black, we are obliged
to use such devices as thickening of lines etc., in order to
show up the tarot satisfactorily.

In recording tarots, they should first be sorted as to
their geometrical forms. Second as to their index line.
The index line of any tarot, is the one, either horizontal
or perpendicular, which contains the Ego or unit, but
NOT the 13. But, of the two such lines, you must take
the one having the smallest numbers next the one. For
instance, take these two lines.. 7 14 22   1 21

12   1 19 22 11

The index line is recorded as: 1 7 14 21 22, no matter
what rotation they come in, in the tarot. Your index
will find the tarot for you in your collection and you
will thus avoid duplication.

Some students prefer to sort only by diagram. Small
collections are as well recorded this way. If the Sun is in
the exact center of a tarot it is called a "Solar Tarot."
if the Sun is in any other square, the tarot is called a
REP. This name comes from the word Republic, on
the theory that the "king" has been set out from his
throne.

A "Straw-stack" is a tarot with a soul which is mixed
in all sorts of inorganic ways. There are many thousands
of this kind in existance.

THE TRANSFORMING OF PYRAMID TAROTS.

This is an important and fascinating science. I shall

attempt to give but a few of the hundreds of transformers in use. To illustrate this art, we take the following diagram:

A	**B**	**C**	**D**	**E**
F	**G**	**H**	**I**	**J**
K	**L**	**M**	**N**	**O**
P	**Q**	**R**	**S**	**T**
U	**V**	**W**	**X**	**Y**

CROSS. Exchange lines A and E, or B and D.

HOP. Exchange lines A and U, or F and P.

Either one of the Crosses plus either one of the Hops, constitutes the General Transformer, known as the Star.

If $A+Y=E+U$, any one of them can be used singly.

JUMP. Exchange lines B and E, or F and U

Either can be used on some tarots and both together on all Q tarots.

STEP. Exchange lines, 1st, AB. 2nd, DE. 3rd, AF. 4th, P and U.

All of these at one time, constitute the General Transformer the "Twist."

1 and 2 alone, or 2 and 4 alone, can be used on any Q Tarot; while some tarots can stand any one of the four steps alone. This kind are called X Tarots.

A "Q" Tarot is one where the quadrilaterals, B F T X M add 65 and the opposite diagonal Quad. the same. An

5	16	20	7	17
4	15	8	14	24
25	23	13	1	3
12	2	18	22	11
19	9	6	21	10

5	7	20	16	17
4	14	8	15	24
25	1	13	23	3
12	22	18	2	11
19	21	6	9	10

4	14	8	15	24
5	7	20	16	17
25	1	13	23	3
12	22	18	2	11
19	21	6	9	10

4	14	8	15	24
12	22	18	2	11
25	1	13	23	3
5	7	20	16	17
19	21	6	9	10

24	14	8	15	4
17	7	20	16	5
3	1	13	23	25
11	22	18	2	12
10	21	6	9	19

14	24	8	4	15
7	17	20	5	16
22	3	13	25	2
1	11	18	12	23
21	10	6	19	9

"X" Tarot is one where A+G=B+F, and so on with all the corners. All Betta Tarots, and many other, have this peculiar quality. The emblem tarot in Chart Two makes the first pair below. The splendid Soul Tarot "Buffalo" is named after the city it was discovered in.

Right JUMP this and we have the well known Alpha; No. 2.

Bottom JUMP No. 1 and we have the sister of Alpha, Miss Betta shown in No. 3.

We can STEP her, as much as we please, without any injury to her soul or her body, as she is a 4X Tarot.

If you Step No. 2, DE PU, you have the wonderful tarot Capri Primo. Step No. 1, PU gives the marvelous and choice "Regulus." We can go on with this process and get numerous other tarots which we have not space to present. X Tarots are great for transforming purposes, as they can be so readily changed to fit odd transformers.

THE THIRD CHART IN THIS SERIES is an inspired tarot made by the writer, in Minneapolis in 1909; with the help of four Inner Temple members. When its beauty was revealed to us by turning over the emblems, we were struck almost dumb by seeing my personal birth elements so emblematically arranged by the Laws of Nature. My birth month doubled; my birth day, 22, stood at each corner faced by my birth year, 44, The strangest thing was the 4 threes, surrounding the sun and one of them, Diamonds, my own birth card. At the top stood three Queens, side by side, while three Jacks stood at the bottom to balance them.

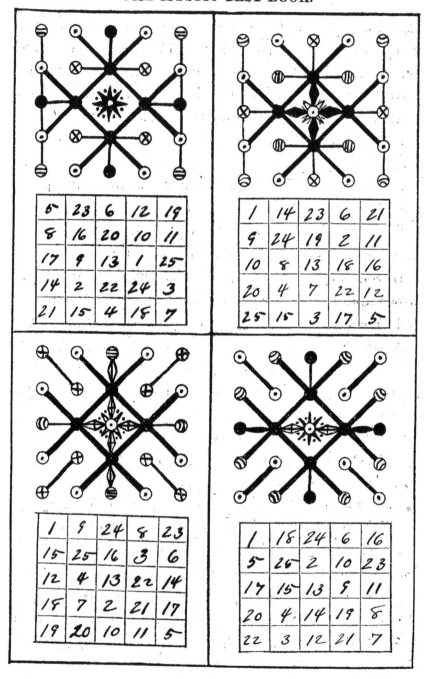

5	23	6	12	19
8	16	20	10	11
17	9	13	1	25
14	2	22	24	3
21	15	4	18	7

1	14	23	6	21
9	24	19	2	11
10	8	13	18	16
20	4	7	22	12
25	15	3	17	5

1	9	24	8	23
15	25	16	3	6
12	4	13	22	14
18	7	2	21	17
19	20	10	11	5

1	18	24	6	16
5	25	2	10	23
17	15	13	9	11
20	4	14	19	8
22	3	12	21	7

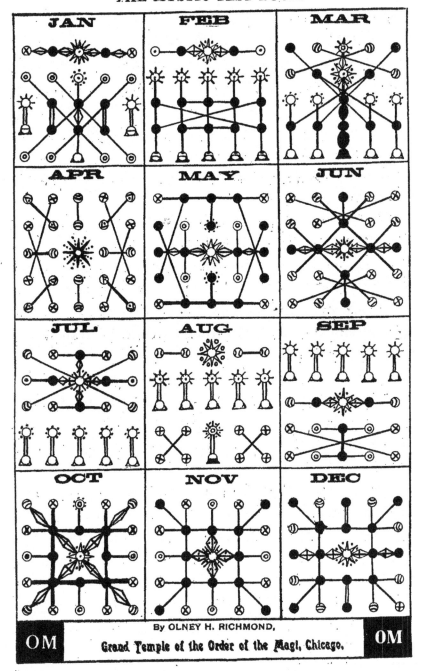

OM

By OLNEY H. RICHMOND,

Grand Temple of the Order of the Magi, Chicago,

OM

At first sight, we thought, with such a lay-out of doubles and birth elements, OM must have sacrificed the tarot to emblemology. But on reading the values, we were astonished to find an entirely new mathematical style of Alpha; an Alpha X Primo. It had the strange quality of the Betta as a 4X Tarot. Right Step this tarot and we have the marvelous Corona, No. 1 on plate. This is a regular formed tarot but hard to diagram in black, as it is so intricate.

CROSS, and we get another Buffalo, with all the qualities of that in Chart Two. Top Step this and we get a Regulus, No. 3. HOP and we have No. 4, our old friend, Betta. STAR and we get No. 5, old Cap. Primo.

During all these changes the birth elements in the original emblem tarot go through wonderful transformations, interesting to view.

CONSIDERATION OF CHART NO. FOUR.

This chart gives only four of the leading Capries, naturally they are all Q Tarots and each is the Leader of several families. Try them with the various transformers given in this book. *Chart No. 5* illustrates the ruling geometric tarot for each month in the year. It is excellent practice, for students, to procure a board and set of blocks and try to discover mathematical tarots to fit some, or all, of these "souls." Blocks, 25 in number, can be purchased in most toy stores. They should be ½" thick; to be handled easily. How to make the best Algebraic Blocks will be taught to sixth degree mystics of the Grand Temple.

CHART NO. 6; gives a few specimens of the celebrated

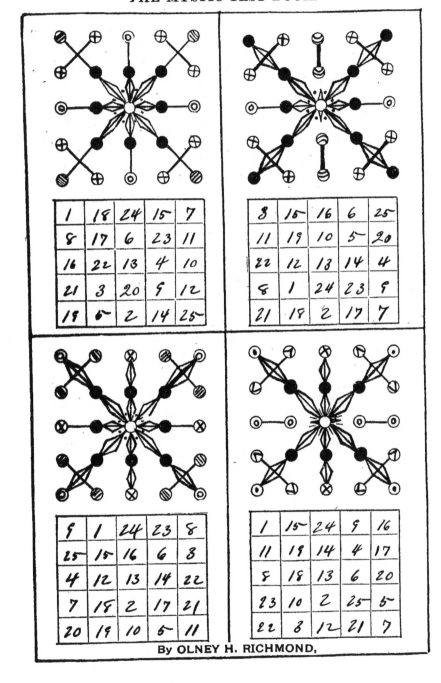

1	18	24	15	7
8	17	6	23	11
16	22	13	4	10
21	3	20	5	12
19	6	2	14	25

3	15	16	6	25
11	19	10	5	20
22	12	13	14	4
8	1	24	23	9
21	18	2	17	7

9	1	24	23	8
25	15	16	6	3
4	12	13	14	22
7	18	2	17	21
20	19	10	5	11

1	15	24	9	16
11	19	14	4	17
5	18	13	6	20
23	10	2	25	5
22	8	12	21	7

By OLNEY H. RICHMOND,

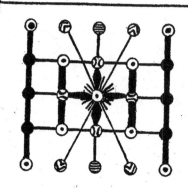

12	22	6	18	7
1	5	24	10	25
23	9	13	17	3
15	21	2	16	11
14	8	20	4	19

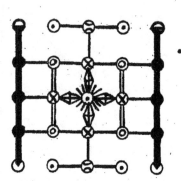

5	1	24	25	10
8	12	20	7	18
9	23	13	8	17
22	14	6	19	4
21	15	2	11	16

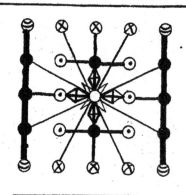

22	1	18	3	21
10	19	15	7	14
17	2	13	24	9
12	20	11	6	16
4	23	8	25	5

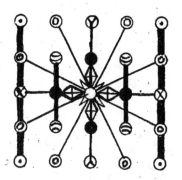

23	12	1	19	10
8	11	5	24	17
22	20	13	6	4
9	15	21	2	18
3	7	25	14	16

ELECTRIC

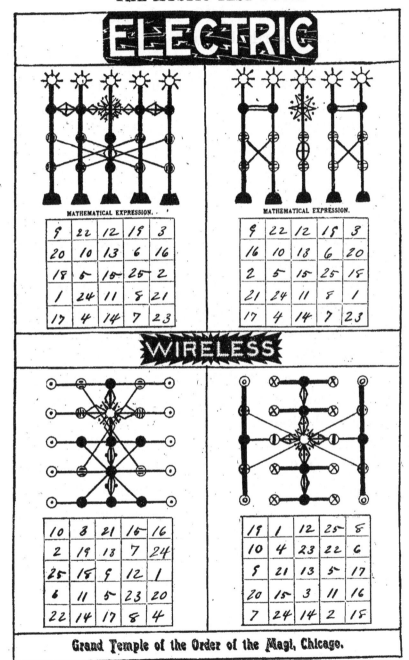

MATHEMATICAL EXPRESSION.

9	22	12	19	3
20	10	13	6	16
18	5	15	25	2
1	24	11	9	21
17	4	14	7	23

MATHEMATICAL EXPRESSION.

9	22	12	19	3
16	10	13	6	20
2	5	15	25	19
21	24	11	9	1
17	4	14	7	23

WIRELESS

10	3	21	19	16
2	19	13	7	24
25	18	9	12	1
6	11	5	23	20
22	14	17	8	4

19	1	12	25	8
10	4	23	22	6
9	21	13	5	17
20	15	3	11	16
7	24	14	2	19

Grand Temple of the Order of the Magi, Chicago.

"Chris" series. These are all Q Tarots and therefore very prolific and well worth the study.

CHART NO. 7; gives a few of the much admired Dorma or "Bedstead" Series. Some of these bedsteads have the strange property of transforming into rooms filled with single beds or cots. I wish I had space to give a few of these; but members can see them in our Temple Archives.

Perhaps this would be as good a place as any, to say that this work is written for and. primarily intended for members of the Order, only. But we do not debar outsiders from buying it and getting what they can out of it.

CHART NO. 8; gives only a few of the four choice Leaders of the great Electric Series. These are the hardest tarots in nature to discover and only a few of them have been made by inspiration. They are best made by using Algebra blocks, and they have to be built up from "cores," the same as building a dynamo. The Sub families are named Electro, Telepher, Wireless, etc. They are individually named after noted electricians.

CHART NO. 9; this illustrates four choice emblematic' tarots, dug from the "depths of the Infinite," by classes of Mystics. The triangles and crosses are of special significance. The "Braider," No. — has been found by two different classes. This kind of tarots are usually recorded in "diamond" form, as the soul is best seen in that position

CHART NO. 10. Number One is another form of the Altar of OM. This one does not have the Sun above it but on its side. Mystics will understand the signification

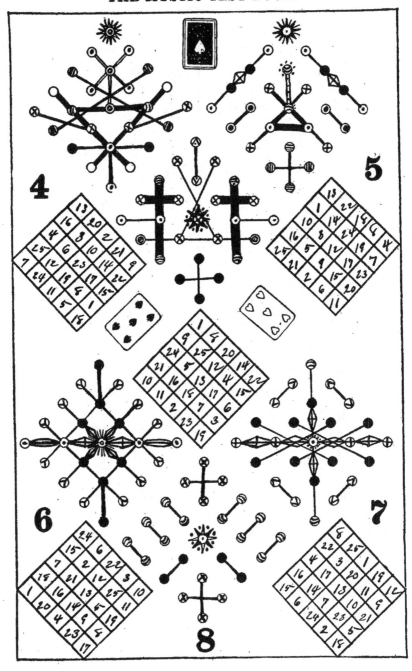

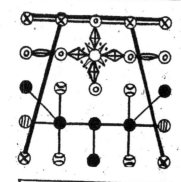

24	15	16	8	2
7	1	13	19	25
3	17	10	21	14
20	23	4	12	6
11	9	22	5	18

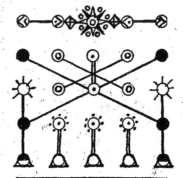

17	21	13	5	9
14	3	19	11	18
4	15	7	23	16
8	20	1	24	12
22	6	25	2	10

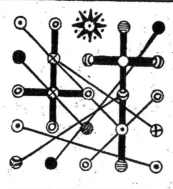

9	2	13	21	20
16	15	22	8	4
25	18	1	14	7
3	24	10	17	11
12	6	19	5	23

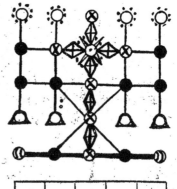

6	12	1	22	24
9	21	13	5	17
23	8	15	16	3
20	14	25	4	2
7	10	11	18	19

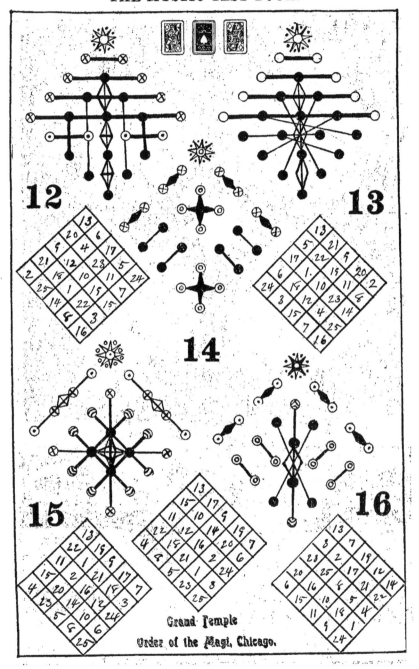

Grand Temple
Order of the Magi, Chicago.

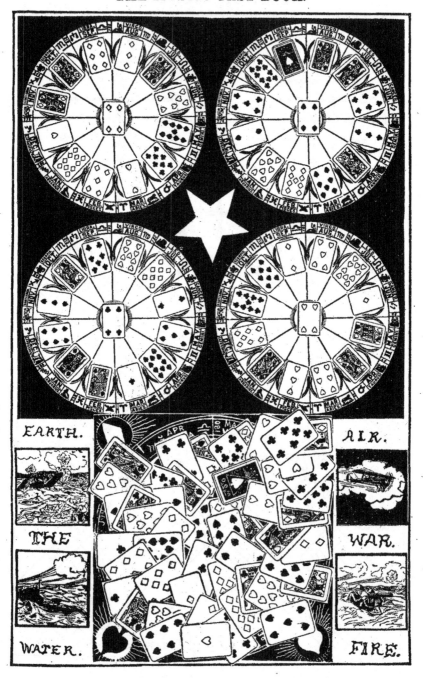

of this. The strange "double cross" was found by a lady from Milwaukee a few years ago. She had two great crosses in her life and one of them had lately been "upset." She admitted this to be strictly true. She was a perfect stranger to me, but the emblems on the Cloth revealed her whole life. She confirmed my interpretation in full.

CHART NO. 11. Tarots number 12 and 13 are members of the famous "Queen" family. They are strange products of Evolution. When four lines of mates are made to run across a tarot diagonally on one-half the tarot, it makes a hard proposition for Nature to fill out the balance, into a perfect tarot. But she was able to do it to a limited extent. Queen number one could not quite come up to the beautiful soul which incarnated in it. It made a good perfect physical tarot, seen below, but this does not balance exactly with the soul above it. The body breeds backs with a sort of avatism to two of its progenitors, and exhibits a peculiar feature of each. But number two has an unbalanced Soul, to conform to its body. Fourteen, Fifteen and Sixteen speak for themselves and are well worth studying.

CHART NO. 12. Many of our higher members have asked for diagrams and directions for finding their entire circle of Birth cards. All persons, except a few born under the Joker or under Fours, have auxiliary birth cards for all the months. The ordinary birth emblem is the basis for finding all of them.

BIRTH EMBLEM ZODIACS.

To find your birth cards for all the houses of the Zodiac:

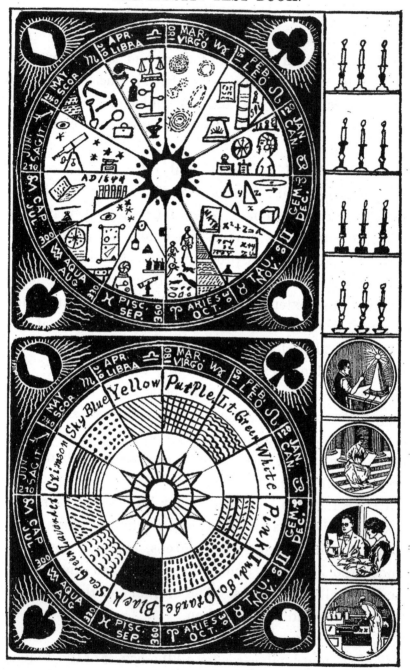

find your ruling birth card in one of the circles and mark that down in the house the Earth was in at your birth. Then take the card next in advance of your card and it is the birth card for the next house and so on. If the birth card is a 4 spot, the person has only one birth emblem for each quarter. They come in the same rotation as shown in the four diagrams. The first diagram is my own birth card circle. All these birth emblems bear peculiar relations to each other and to the regular birth card. Below these diagrams we give a "conglomerate" of the Test Book, the emblems being thrown on in a promiscuous manner. This particular one represented the late war and was spread in 1914. Such lay-outs are full of meaning to those who understand reading them. Many persons, some of them outsiders, have noticed that this War covered the FOUR Elements, Fire, Water, Earth and Air. This is illustrated in the plate. Will this be the last great war? We sincerely hope so.

CHART NO. 13. The first Zodiac ilustrates the "Twelve Lights of Science" by emblems of Art and Craft. The second Zodiac gives the color of the twelve houses and illustrates at the side, Light; Wisdom; Trade and Labor of the Four Quarters.

If we had a full circle of twelve temples, the various houses would be draped at the doors and windows in those colors, and the charts of each degree would be hung upon the walls. Such a city as Chicago should have a million dollar temple furnished in accordance with this plan.

ORDER OF THE MAGI,

This Order is a true *Secret Order* in the fullest sense of the word. Its very cause of existence, its importance and its foundation principles are strictly secret and are obliged to be so from the very nature of things.

But the *Religion of the Stars*, which is the religion of the Order, *is not secret*. Its preachings and its practice is open to all who can appreciate it. The secret machinery of the Order is simply the vehicle by which the religion is taught and exploited in its various degrees according to the universal *law of evolution*.

Those who would know more regarding this ancient Order, can obtain information in the form of bulletins, circulars, papers, etc., at any time in the future, by sending address and stamps to

O. H. RICHMOND,

The Grand Temple is located at this date,